The Pretender

JUAN RUIZ DE ALARCÓN

The Pretender, or A Man Beside Himself

Translated by

The UCLA Working Group
on the *Comedia* in Translation and Performance:

Marta Albalá Pelegrín   Javier Patiño Loira
Paul Fitzgibbon Cella   Amanda Riggle
Barbara Fuchs   Kenneth Sánchez
Rafael Jaime   Rhonda Sharrah
Brenda Jaramillo   Cheché Silveyra
Rachel Kaufman   Aina Soley Mateu
Robin Kello   Samantha Solis
Laura Muñoz   Veronica Toro

Juan de la Cuesta
Newark, Delaware

Juan de la Cuesta Hispanic Monographs
An imprint of LinguaText, LLC
103 Walker Way
Newark, Delaware 19711 USA
(302) 453-8695

www.JuandelaCuesta.com

MANUFACTURED IN THE UNITED STATES OF AMERICA
ISBN: 978-1-58871-396-4 (PB)

Table of Contents

The *Comedia* in Context

The "Golden Age" of Spain offers one of the most vibrant theatrical repertoires ever produced. At the same time that England saw the flourishing of Shakespeare on the Elizabethan stage, Spain produced prodigious talents such as Lope de Vega, Tirso de Molina, and Calderón de la Barca. Although those names may not resonate with the force of the Bard in the Anglophone world, the hundreds of entertaining, complex plays they wrote, and the stage tradition they helped develop, deserve to be better known.

The *Diversifying the Class*ics project at UCLA brings these plays to the public by offering English versions of Hispanic classical theater. Our translations are designed to make this rich tradition accessible to students, teachers, and theater professionals. This brief introduction to the *comedia* in its context suggests what we might discover and create when we begin to look beyond Shakespeare.

Comedia at a Glance

The Spanish *comedia* developed in the late sixteenth and early seventeenth centuries. As Madrid grew into a sophisticated imperial capital, the theater provided a space to perform the customs, concerns, desires, and anxieties of its citizens. Though the form was influenced by the Italian troupes that brought *commedia dell'arte* to Spain in the sixteenth century, the expansive corpus of the Spanish *comedia* includes not only comic plays, but also histories, tragedies, and tragicomedies. The varied dramatic template of the *comedia* is as diverse as the contemporary social sphere it reflects.

While the plays offer a range of dramatic scenarios and theatrical effects, they share structural and linguistic similarities. Roughly three thousand lines, they are usually divided into three different *jornadas*, or acts. Plots move quickly across time and space, without much regard for the Aristotelian unities of action, time, and place. The plays are written in verse, and employ different forms for different characters and situations: a lover may deliver an ornate sonnet in honor of the beloved, while a servant offers a shaggy-dog story in rhymed couplets. The plays' language is designed for the ear rather than the eye, with the objective of pleasing an audience.

The *comedia* was performed in rectangular courtyard spaces known as *corrales*. Built between houses of two or three stories, the *corral* offered seating based on social position, including space for the nobles in the balconies, women in the *cazuela*, or stewpot, and *mosqueteros*, or groundlings, on patio benches. This cross-section of society enjoyed a truly popular art, which reflected onstage their varied social positions. A *comedia* performance would have included the play as well as songs, dances, and *entremeses*, or short comic interludes, before, after, and between the acts. As the first real commercial theater, the corral was the place where a diverse urban society found its dramatic entertainment.

What's at Stake on the *Comedia* Stage?

Comedias offer a range of possibilities for the twenty-first century reader, actor, and audience. The plays often envision the social ambitions and conflicts of the rapidly-growing cities where they were performed, allowing a community to simultaneously witness and create a collective culture. In many *comedias*, the anonymity and wealth that the city affords allow the clever to transcend their social position, while wit, rather than force, frequently carries the day, creating an urban theater that itself performs urbanity. An important subset of *comedias* deal with topics from national history, exploring violence, state power, the role of the nobility, and religious and racial difference.

The *comedia* often examines social hierarchies that may be less rigid than they first appear. Whether the dominant mode of the play is comic, tragic, historical, or a mixture, its dramatic progression often depends on a balancing act of order and liberty, authority and transgression, stasis and transformation. The title of Lope de Vega's recently rediscovered *Women and Servants*, in which two sisters scheme to marry the servant-men they love rather than the noblemen who woo them, makes explicit its concerns with gender and class and provides a view of what is at stake in many of the plays. Individuals disadvantaged by class or gender often challenge the social hierarchy and patriarchy by way of their own cleverness. The *gracioso* (comic sidekick), the *barba* (older male blocking figure), and the lovers appear repeatedly in these plays, and yet are often much more than stock types. At their most remarkable, they reflect larger cultural possibilities. The *comedia* stages the conflicting demands of desire and reputation, dramatizing the tension between our identities as they are and as we wish them to be.

Among the many forms of passion and aspiration present in the *comedia*, female desire and agency are central. In contrast to its English counterpart, the Spanish stage permitted actresses to play female roles, thus giving playwrights the opportunity to develop a variety of characters for them. While actresses became famous, the powerful roles they played onstage often portrayed the force of female desire. In Lope's *The Widow of Valencia*, for example, the beautiful young widow Leonarda brings a masked lover into her home so as not to reveal her identity and risk her reputation or independence.

The presence of actresses, however, did not diminish the appeal of the cross-dressing plot. One of Tirso's most famous plays, *Don Gil of the Green Breeches*, features Doña Juana assuming a false identity and dressing as a man in order to foil the plans of her former lover, who is also in disguise. Dizzying deceptions and the performance of identity are both dramatic techniques and thematic concerns in these plays. Gender, like class, becomes part of the structure the *comedia* examines and dismantles, offering a powerful reflection on how we come to be who we are.

Remaking Plays in Our Time

In Lope's witty manifesto, the *New Art of Making Plays in Our Time*, he advises playwrights to stick to what works onstage, including plots of honor and love, strong subplots, and—whenever possible—cross-dressing. For Lope, the delight of the audience drives the process of composition, and there is little sense in a craft that does not entertain the public. Lope's contemporaries followed this formula, developing dramas that simultaneously explore the dynamics of their society and produce spectacle. For this reason, early modern Hispanic drama remains an engaging, suspenseful, often comic—and new—art to audiences even four hundred years later.

The *Diversifying the Classics* project at UCLA, engaged in translation, adaptation, and outreach to promote the *comedia* tradition, aims to bring the entertaining spirit of Lope and his contemporaries to our work. Rather than strictly adhering to the verse forms of the plays, we seek to render the power of their language in a modern idiom; rather than limiting the drama as a historical or cultural artifact, we hope to bring out what remains vibrant for our contemporary society. Given that these vital texts merit a place onstage, we have sought to facilitate production by carefully noting entrances, exits, and asides, and by adding locations for scenes whenever possible. Although we have translated every line, we assume directors will cut as appropriate for their own productions. We hope that actors, directors, and readers will translate our work further into new productions, bringing both the social inquiry and theatrical delight of the *comedia* to future generations of audiences.

A Note on the Playwright

Juan Ruiz de Alarcón (1580?-1639) is one of the central figures of Spanish classical theater and a foundational influence on the related French corpus. He was born in the viceroyalty of New Spain—either in the silver mines of Taxco or in Mexico City—to Spanish parents who had come to America shortly after the fall of Mexico-Tenochtitlan, the Aztec capital, to an army of Castilian explorers, West African slaves, and Native American warriors in 1521. Alarcón crossed the Atlantic on three occasions: in 1600, he traveled to the University of Salamanca to finish the studies in canon and civil law that he had begun at the Royal and Pontifical University of Mexico; in 1608, in a voyage that some critics believe inspired *The Pretender*, he returned to Mexico City, where he worked for the government; in 1613, he returned to Spain and settled in Madrid, launching his career as playwright and finally as civil servant for the Council of the Indies.

Compared to other playwrights of his time, Alarcón's corpus is small. He published his collected *comedias*, 20 in total, in two volumes, one in 1628 and the other in 1634. Among his most famous plays is *La verdad sospechosa*. This hilarious *comedia* of a pathological liar was well received in Spain and widely celebrated by the French. Pierre Corneille translated it as *Le Menteur* and it was first presented on the French stage in 1644. Molière, another towering figure in French classical theater, staged *Le Menteur* several times between 1659 and 1664. Voltaire famously wrote: "it is probably to this translation [of Alarcón's *La verdad sospechosa*] that we owe Molière." To this day, *La verdad sospechosa* is frequently produced, in a testament to its appeal for audiences. Corneille's *Le Menteur*, now translated into English by David Ives, premiered at the Shakespeare Theater Company under the direction of Michael Kahn in 2010. It has since been staged in Los Angeles, Portland, Westport, Santa Cruz, and New York. Dakin Matthews translated Alarcón's original as *The Truth Can't Be Trusted, or The Liar.* It premiered in Los Angeles in 2000 and is included in Juan de la Cuesta's *The Comedia in Translation and Performance* series.

Alarcón lived at a time and in a world of constant and profound changes and transformations. In the past, critics debated whether he was Spanish or Mexican. In truth, he was both and neither. He is, in fact, an early example of the *criollo/creole*, a person of European descent fundamentally marked by his upbringing among Native Americans and Spaniards, African and Asian servants, traders, and communities of enslaved people, in a city peppered with European merchants of all nations. Alarcón was the product of a society that was as complex and varied as any of our modern megalopolises. He was truly a global playwright.

Introduction
Cheché Silveyra

A STRANGE NEW WORLD: THE PLOT DEVICE

AMONG THE THOUSANDS OF *comedias* composed during the Hispanic Golden Age, *The Pretender* stands alone. The action is motivated by one of the strangest plot devices found in a work of fiction, as the limits of disguise and identity are taken to disconcerting extremes. Set in the city of Seville, the play begins with a suspicion: Juan, the protagonist, decides to test the loyalty of his beloved, Ana, by pretending to be Diego, a cousin of his from Flanders.[1] To this end, Juan circulates two false documents. The first is a letter to his father, in which "Diego" declares his intention to visit Seville in order to witness what he has only heard in rumors: that he and his cousin look exactly the same. The second is a portrait of Juan, but with the image identified as Diego's. The cogs are put in motion as Juan pretends to leave for Peru at the same time as the false Diego is to arrive in Seville for his visit. Once the pieces of this complicated hoax are in place, all that Juan needs to do is change his name to Diego and present himself to family and servants as if he were a completely different person. Against all logic, the plan works. Everyone in his immediate circle—his love interest, his father, his lifelong servant—accept that this man is who he says he is, which is to say cousin Diego from Flanders, even though a few days before he was living among them as Juan and he still looks exactly like his old self.

Costume was a dramatic device as popular among early modern Hispanic playwrights and audiences as it was contentious among critics. Peninsular audiences—organized in strict social classes both within and beyond the *corral de comedias*—enthusiastically received plays in which the dramatic conflict was driven by characters who, hiding behind a mask or veil and ap-

---

1   Spain ruled much of what is today the Netherlands and Brussels in the period. "Spanish Flanders" was the name used for this territory.

propriating dress codes typically reserved for others, pretended to be what they were not.[2] Lope de Vega, who revolutionized the *comedia*, had recognized early on that audiences loved female characters cross-dressed as male. In his groundbreaking poetics, *Arte nuevo de hacer comedias* (New Art of Writing Plays, 1609), Lope recommended the use of cross-dressing, but with decorum. Of course, much of the point of cross-dressing was the access it provided to female bodies: while traditional female dress was designed to conceal the body under its wide and loose shape, male attire was comprised of snug fitting doublets and revealing tight breeches.

Playwrights used the trope of the cross-dressed woman to explore the borders of gender and its performative nature, as is the case of *Don Gil de las calzas verdes* (Don Gil of the Green Breeches, ca. 1615), by Tirso de Molina, and of *Valor, agravio y mujer* (ca. 1630), by Ana Caro, recently translated by our group as *The Courage to Right a Woman's Wrongs*.[3] In play after play, disguises proved to be effective and flexible dramatic devices: in Lope's *El perro del hortelano* (The Dog in the Manger, 1613), it is enough for the servant Tristán to don some exotic fabrics and a turban to pass for a rich Greek merchant; in Calderón de la Barca's *Amar después de la muerte* (ca. 1650), translated by our group as *To Love Beyond Death*, the Morisco warrior Tuzaní passes for an Old Christian soldier by dressing in their fashion.[4] Disguises, then, could fulfill a number of dramatic functions and take multiple forms, but they always involved a visual transformation. What sets *The Pretender* apart is that the only disguise the protagonist takes on, among his nearest and dearest, is a name change.

It has been suggested that *Pretender* is informed by *Menaechmi*, a play by the Roman author Plautus, in which it is impossible to distinguish between two identical twins of the same name who were separated at birth (Millares Carlo 349). But there are no twins in *Pretender*. In fact, Juan and Diego share the stage for most of the play under feigned identities, and there is no indication that the rest of cast ever confuses them with one another due to their physical similarities. The fact is that these two don't look alike at all, which is

---

2   *Corrales de comedias* were open air theaters constructed between buildings two or three stories high. Women and men were assigned to different zones at the lower levels, while nobles watched from special rooms above.

3   The *Comedia* in Translation research group makes its translations and critical studies freely available to the public on their website http://diversifyingtheclassics.humanities.ucla.edu.

4   *Morisco* was a blanket term applied to Iberian Muslims who were converted, often by force, to Christianity.

why Juan was compelled to produce the false portrait and craft the fake story of his resemblance to Diego. Neither is it a matter of homonymy or doppelgängers: in *Pretender*, there is only one body, that of Juan, in which two identities coexist, his own and Diego's. The change of name is the entirety of a disguise that, in dissimulating the identity of Juan, simulates that of Diego.

Like so many *comedias* from the period, *Pretender* presents the idea that identity is a social construct: Juan may pretend to be Diego as much as he wants, but in order to be successful, his transformation must be approved by the group. In the many plays mentioned above, a change in identity comes from hiding or transforming identifying marks, with materiality playing an essential role: a pair of breeches and a sword are necessary artifacts for, say, a woman named Leonor to become a man named Leonardo, as in Ana Caro's *Courage*. Yet in *Pretender*, the transformation of Juan into Diego takes place without a change in legible identity marks. That such an extreme yet superficial transformation creates no resistance among Juan's closest circle might lead us interpret the plot device as silly, a contrivance or caprice on the part of the playwright. But more interesting possibilities emerge when we take into account the highly complex and ever-changing society of Alarcón's time.

Alarcón's world was in constant transformation. Advances in science and technology, changes in the political landscape, the rapid spread of unknown diseases, were—as they remain to this day—constant reminders that what we know about our world or ourselves is always partial and momentary. The arrival of the Castilians in America in 1492 demonstrated that the Earth was much larger than previously thought: a whole new world, full of wealth, adventure, and possibilities, lay across the Atlantic. For those like Alarcón, living in the late 16th and early 17th centuries, the Earth had been reshaped. Their world was, in a sense, brand new. As the massive Castilian empire came into being, traditional ideas of identity were suddenly challenged by the sweeping presence of diversity. Beyond its eccentricities, what *Pretender*'s peculiar plot device reveals is an attempt at bringing onto the stage the realities of a strange new world.

THE PLOTS

Act I. The play begins as Don Juan de Castro, the protagonist, lays out his complicated plans to change identities to his close friend Leonardo. Juan's cousin Ana, recently orphaned, has been brought by Don Rodrigo, Juan's father, to live among them, and Juan has fallen madly in love with her. When Juan's father sends him to Lima to claim an inheritance, Juan senses treachery: either his father doesn't think that Juan is a suitable match for Ana, or, even worse, his father wants her for himself. Juan's solution is to spy on them by continuing to live with his father and beloved without being recognized by either. To achieve this, Juan has secured the help of his cousin, Don Diego de Luján, who grew up in Flanders and just recently moved to Madrid. The plan is to spin the tale that these two cousins look exactly the same, so that Juan can pretend to be Diego. To this end, Juan has asked Diego to send to send a letter to Rodrigo, Juan's father, stating his curiosity about their uncanny similarity, and to accompany the letter with a portrait of Juan, but labeled as Diego. In support of this charade, Juan will pretend to travel to Peru with Leonardo, who will, in turn, pretend to be Juan for the rest of the voyage, because as soon as the ship sets sail Juan will return to shore on a hired boat. Back on land, he will adopt the identity of Diego and present himself to his father and beloved as if he were a completely different man.

Leonardo and Julia, who were once lovers, are meeting in her house at her request. Believing that Julia wants to rekindle their old flame, Leonardo rejects her in a cruel exchange. Julia first pretends not to care for him, then finally admits to feelings for him and requests that he stay in Seville, but Leonardo refuses to break his promise to Juan to go to Peru in his stead. When Juan walks on stage, Julia asks if he would be willing to release Leonardo from his bond, to which Juan agrees. Yet Leonardo, arguing that his friend needs him, and that love should not overcome friendship, insists his promise be upheld.

The bickering is interrupted when Gerardo announces that Celio, Julia's brother, has just arrived. Julia, feeling compromised by the men's presence in her house, fears her brother's reaction. However, Juan swiftly comes up with the lie that he and Leonardo were merely passing by to say farewell, as they are both leaving for Peru.

Act II. Juan walks on stage as Sancho is describing the royal fleet on which his master—the very same Juan who just entered the stage—supposedly left for Peru earlier that same day. According to Juan, the galleons were so old and battered that they barely made it to Lisbon, from where he took the road back to Seville. Sancho suspects that this man is, in fact, the cousin Diego de Luján pretending to be his master: "It's his face and voice, / Inés, but I don't recognize those clothes / or his beard, or anything else. / Don Juan's beard is not so full" (lines 1090-4). The servant changes his own name to test the real identity of this suspect figure: Sancho presents himself as Philandro, then as Armindo, and, encountering no resistance, decides that this person is, in fact, Diego de Luján trying to pass for Juan, which is immediately confirmed by

Juan himself: "I wanted to see / if the resemblance between / Don Juan and myself / was as strong as people claim. / Having fooled his father, / I see that I am exactly like him" (lines 1112-7). The lingering skepticism of Don Rodrigo, Juan's father, is assuaged when he realizes that the clothes that Juan is wearing are a perfect match to those in the portrait falsely identified as Diego's. And so Don Rodrigo welcomes this false Diego into his home, inviting him to stay indefinitely.

Juan, acting as Diego, strikes up a flattering conversation with Ana. The real Diego, having arrived alongside Juan, is on stage passing for a servant named Mendo. Juan tells Mendo that he finds Ana too receptive to his faked persona, to which Mendo replies: "Well, what are you after? / Are you jealous of yourself?" Juan answers: "Why not? If she embraces me as Don Diego, / does she not offend me as Don Juan?" (lines 1174-7). Juan also wants to test the loyalty of his servant, and so, acting as Diego, he offers Sancho a bribe. When Sancho tells him that he is watching over Ana for his master, Juan makes him a proposition: if, against his master's wishes, Sancho helps this false Diego in his pursuit of Ana, Sancho will be compensated. Sancho agrees and Juan reveals his identity. Faced with his master's anger, Sancho explains that he took Diego's money, but planned to betray him by remaining loyal to Juan. Then Juan reverses identity once more, and, claiming to be Diego, calls Sancho a liar and a traitor. "Go away!" responds Sancho, "By my life! / Will this go on all day? / 'I'm Don Diego' and 'I'm Don Juan'" (lines 1336-8). Vowing not to serve either Juan or Diego, the bewildered Sancho leaves the stage.

In Celio's house, Gerardo tries to force himself on Julia. She screams for help and her brother rushes in sword in hand. Julia explains that Gerardo had pretended to be Celio's friend in order to gain access to the house and offend her. Once Julia leaves, Gerardo lies to Celio, saying that he has been properly courting Julia for a long time, but that she has shown favor to the newly arrived Diego de Luján. Gerardo claims that he came to the house to break up with Julia, but she, feeling offended, falsely accused him of compromising her honor. The scene comes to an end as Celio promises to investigate further.

Outside Celio's house, Juan and Sancho are having an argument: Inés has fallen for Mendo, who is actually the real Diego, and now Sancho, jealous of Mendo, wants Juan to dismiss Mendo in exchange for Sancho's help with Ana. As Sancho leaves the stage, Mendo enters. He falls in love with Julia as soon as he sees her and begins to follow her mindlessly, leaving Juan behind.

Back in Don Rodrigo's house, Diego explains his history with Julia. As a boy he went to Flanders to serve a nobleman, whose wife, in turn, employed Julia. Diego and Julia fell in love, but when her brother, Celio, had to return to Spain, he took her with him. Diego tried to leave Flanders, to no avail. Then, when Diego had at last concocted a plan to leave for Spain, he heard news that Celio and Julia had drowned trying to cross a river. Now, after many years, he has found her alive and well, living in Seville. But there is one problem: Julia is now in love with Leonardo, who took Juan's place in the trip to Peru. Juan is therefore obliged to look after Leonardo's interests and asks Diego to renounce Julia. Enraged, Diego leaves the stage with a warning: "I will tear out the very soul of one / who seeks to take mine from me" (lines 1745-6).

Juan is beginning to understand the implications of the web of lies that he has conceived as Inés walks in, asking why Mendo (Diego), looked so upset. Juan explains that he dismissed him on account of Inés: he begged Mendo to love her, but he would not budge. Inés wants Juan to reinstate Mendo and then to marry them. When Juan says that the matter is beyond his authority, Inés replies: "I suggest you see to this. / For if you don't do as I wish, / I will tell my master Don Rodrigo / that you are wooing his niece" (lines 1796-9).

Just then, Ana walks in. Every day she finds Juan, who is acting as Diego, more attractive. Ana offers him encouragement: "disdain is just a step along the way / for one who prevails in the end" (lines 1839-40). Juan tells her that a change of heart does not reflect fickleness on her part, yet when Ana admits that she has fallen for him, he flies off the handle and reveals his true identity. But Juan's lies have emboldened others to lie as well, so Ana responds that she was merely punishing him for lying to her in order to test her loyalty: "I spoke those words to you, / whether you call yourself Diego or Juan. / A change in name / does not change the substance. / I have loved the same body and soul / all along. How could I have betrayed / you with yourself?" (lines 1932-8). Juan is not convinced, but Ana will have no more of his lies: "If you're Don Diego, / my love is yours, have no fear, / but if you're Don Juan, then by God, / it's off to Lima with you!" (lines 1960-3).

Act III. Juan, acting as Diego, meets with Celio at Don Rodrigo's house. Celio says that he knew a Diego de Luján in Flanders who looked nothing like him. Juan's response adds another lie to his already complicated scheme: that the Diego de Luján whom Celio met in the Netherlands is *also* a cousin of his, adding another Diego de Luján to the mix. But the real reason why

Celio wants to speak to Juan is to warn him: if Juan's intentions towards Julia are honorable, then he should ask for her hand in marriage; otherwise, Celio will resort to arms to protect his family honor. Juan lies, stating that he has never set foot in Celio and Julia's house. Now Ana, who has overheard the conversation, suspects that Juan is two-timing her with Julia. Ana orders Inés to hide in Juan's bed-curtains so that she can spy on his conversations with Mendo. Meanwhile, Ana will confront Juan in order to distract him: she knows that he is, in fact, Diego, a dishonest man whom she cannot love—she loves Juan and was only interested in Diego because of their similarities.

Juan and Sancho are complaining about what they claim is women's fickleness and susceptibility to gold. Sancho worries that Mendo is pursuing Inés, but Juan assures him that he has nothing to fear and invites him to hide in an adjacent room so that he can secretly listen to what he and Mendo have to say about the matter. Sancho finds a casket of wine in his hiding place and drinks it. As Juan and Mendo speak, Sancho, drunk, falls asleep and begins to snore. Violently woken by Mendo, Sancho jumps to his feet, in the process ripping the bed-curtains behind which Inés was hiding.

In Celio's house, Diego finds Julia writing a letter to Leonardo. She recognizes Diego as her old lover from her days in Flanders, but Diego, jealous because she is writing a letter to another man, berates her and leaves. She orders her servant to follow Diego but is told that the man who just left is Mendo, servant to a Diego de Luján who is staying at Don Rodrigo's house. Julia goes to Don Rodrigo's, finding Juan and Diego. Since Diego has rudely accused her of fickleness, she wants to set the record straight: since she returned from Flanders seven years ago, she never once received a letter from Diego, which led her to believe that she had been forgotten: "In the absence of all hope, / I took on a new love. / It's not fickleness to seek / a port in a storm" (lines 2651-4). While Diego was away, Julia fell in love with Leonardo, but now she loves Diego again. At this moment, Leonardo arrives. Juan asks Julia to hide while he figures out why Leonardo is back from Peru so soon. Leonardo relates how he slipped off his ship into icy waters, only to be rescued by another ship and brought him back to Europe, without him ever reaching Peru. The situation is further complicated as Celio, led by Gerardo, appears demanding that his sister be handed over to him immediately, or he will burn down the house.

Don Rodrigo enters, startled by the commotion. Celio explains the situation to Rodrigo, who decides he will make Juan marry Julia to restore Celio's honor. When Rodrigo returns with Julia, Juan explains that he has no interest in her and, thus, has not damaged her honor: Julia is at his house looking for news of Leonardo. Celio then turns to Leonardo and demands that *he* marry Julia instead. Yet the real Diego will not see his beloved Julia married to another man, even if it means exposing all of Juan's deceptions: he explains that he and Julia have been in love for years, and that he has been playing along with Juan, but must now break his silence, lest he lose Julia. Juan admits to his lies: he just wanted to test Ana's loyalty. Ana explains that she cannot betray Juan with himself—she loves him and a change of name cannot change the way she feels for him. The last lie of the play comes from Ana, who claims that she knew from the start that the man pretending to be Diego was, in fact, Juan. His doubts assuaged, Juan gives his hand to Ana and the play comes to an end.

NEW WORLDS, NEW FACES: DIVERSITY IN THE CASTILIAN EMPIRE
After the arrival of the Spaniards on the island of Hispaniola in 1492, Castile's territories grew exponentially: in just a few decades, it became a worldwide empire, with colonies in America, Asia, Africa, and Europe connecting the world like never before. On the Manila-Acapulco route, established in the 1560s, wealth of all kinds traveled on Spanish galleons from the Philippines to the west coast of Mexico, then was transported by land to Mexico City, the viceregal capital, before making its way to Spain. Products of Asian origin—rice, ceramics, decorative screen folds, to name just a few—swiftly became staples of Novohispanic—meaning "from New Spain," as Mexico was then known to Spaniards—and later Mexican culture.

The convergence in Mexico City of peoples and cultures from around the world created profound and permanent changes on the landscape of New Spain. And yet, having reached Mexico City, the royal cargo from Asian territories had merely completed half its voyage. As it moved eastward through New Spain, the royal cargo was augmented with American wealth until it finally reached the port of Veracruz, in the Gulf of Mexico, from where it was shipped to Seville for distribution throughout the Iberian Peninsula and other European territories. Eventually, American products like tomatoes, chilies, and chocolate—names that derive from Nahuatl, the language of the Aztecs or Mexicas—as well as vanilla, tobacco, and cochineal red dye—a vibrant pigment employed in masterworks from Rubens to van Gogh—reached Europe and were permanently adopted by its peoples. Enslaved indigenous subjects also made it to the shores of Spain. It is estimated that around 650,000 people were enslaved and forced to relocate throughout the transatlantic world, of which about 2500 left legal traces that place them in the Kingdom of Castile (Van Deusen 2). The inhabitants of the Spanish city of Seville, where *Pretender* is set, gradually began to encounter in their streets and homes peoples and languages they had never experienced before: indigenous Maya and native Filipinos, to name but two possibilities, would intermingle in the streets of Seville with Christian servants—including the descendants of Iberian Muslims now forcefully converted to Catholicism—and a longstanding, "infinite multitude" of Africans.[5] If Spain was a world-wide empire, it only makes sense that its subjects and their cultures would be as diverse as the world was wide.

In due time, the galleons returned to the colonies and did so loaded with people. Over 200,000 Europeans had moved to the Americas by 1600 (Pastor 49), including merchants, notaries, judges, and lawyers (Brading 39). On at least one occasion, Alarcón was among them, and *Pretender* depicts such a voyage. The realism and historical accuracy of the description, in a play so full of eccentricities, has stood out for critics, some of whom claim that *Pretender* must be Alarcón's first play, written in New Spain around the year 1608 (Millares 22-3). Although it is not accepted by all scholars, this argument suggests that the diverse population of New Spain, comprised of American Indians, Africans, Asians, Europeans, and all the possible combinations afforded by practices of *mestizaje*—the biological and cultural mixing of ethnicities—led Alarcón to reflect on identity in his play.

The mention in *Pretender* of several Castilian colonies—Flanders, Peru, Mexico—and of an array of unorthodox identities—Indios, Moriscos, Jews—even if oblique and of no dramatic relevance, paradoxically place the margins of the empire at the center. As subjects and cultures the world over populate the city of Seville, *Pretender* becomes a site of contestation where traditional notions of identity must confront diversity: who is a Spaniard, and what makes them so? What makes us "us," and what makes "them" something different?

STRANGERS FROM WITHIN: PRACTICES OF ACCULTURATION
Pretender begins as Juan, the protagonist, and Leonardo, his close friend, enter the stage discussing what deserves to be named the world's eight wonder.[6] While Juan proposes Seville, Leonardo makes a case for the Mexican drain, a

---

5   In the middle of the 1500s, Luis de Peraza wrote: "There is an infinite multitude of black men and women from all parts of Ethiopia and Guinea who are our servants in Seville and are brought here by way of Portugal" (134; translation mine).

6   The expression describes a structure as magnificent as the seven wonders of the classical world, which traditionally included the Great Pyramid of Giza, the Lighthouse of Alexandria, the Colossus of Rhodes, etc.

titanic project of hydraulic engineering devised to empty the system of lakes that surrounded the island of Mexico-Tenochtitlan, which by Alarcón's time had become Mexico City and the capital of New Spain.[7] In order to control the devastating floods that brought the capital to its knees every few years, the viceroy decided to drain the lakes. Bringing the project to fruition demanded tunneling through mountains and carving channels to redirect the water to a river that drained out into the Gulf of Mexico.[8]

In the play, Leonardo relates the history of the Mexican drain in a long monologue without an evident dramatic purpose. The opening lines are telling:

> The city of Mexico,
> the celebrated head of the Indian world,
> which is called New Spain,... (lines 45-7)[9]

The city of Mexico-Tenochtitlan was the center of the Mexica empire, a powerful political network that, at the arrival of the Spaniards in 1519, dominated large swaths of the region known today as Mesoamerica.[10] At this time, Mexico-Tenochtitlan was ruled by the legendary Moctezuma, the *tlatoani*, or king, of the Mexica people. In recent years, historians have challenged the idea that the Spanish conquest destroyed the Mexica civilization: "while Tenochtitlan as an indigenous imperial capital certainly came to an end with its conquest, the death of Tenochtitlan as an indigenous city is a myth...[I]ndigenous Tenochtitlan lived on" (Mundy 3). Native structures, both material and political, remained functional and were employed by the viceregal administration for centuries. The native population remained under the government of

---

7   Mexico-Tenochtitlan, the Aztec capital, was built on a small island in a large system of interconnected lakes. The word Aztec is an exonym. The people who built this city called themselves Mexica (Meh-SHEE-kah).

8   The waters finally stopped flowing in the early 20th century. As the lakes were drained out, the aquatic environment of Mexico-Tenochtitlan also disappeared.

9   Gladys Robalino has called attention to how Leonardo, in his description of Mexico as the "head of the Indian world," highlights its primacy in relation to the rest of the American territories. In this way, the city was a place of indigenous authority that would have to be removed before being replaced by the Castilian one: the substitution of the name "Indian world" for that of "New Spain" marks the new condition of subordination.

10   Mesoamerica is a historical and cultural area extending from central Mexico to northern Costa Rica. It has been inhabited by an array of Native American societies since at least 1200 BCE

indigenous dynastic governors, operating in the Nahuatl language and using the Mesoamerican writing system in legal suits, local histories and other cultural expressions. In the years that Alarcón lived in New Spain, roughly from 1580 to 1613, both cities—Nahua Tenochtitlan and Castilian Mexico—visibly coexisted on the singular, physical space of a tiny island, much like in *Pretender* the identities of Juan and Diego coexist in the single body of the duplicitous protagonist. Overlapping identities, it turns out, were not a new concept for Alarcón.

At the individual level, these overlapping identities were even more pronounced. Mass baptisms of Native American subjects to the Catholic faith began soon after the conquest. As the new converts were inscribed in the ecclesiastical records under traditional Spanish names, their colonial identities were officially fixed. Nevertheless, the indigenous population continued to use their own native names in their communities (Cline 479; Horn 113). A good example are the Nahua noblemen in charge of governing the indigenous populations.[11] These men ruled according to traditional native politics, were known by their native names, and participated in native celebrations sanctioned by both the Catholic church and the Castilian administration.[12] Among the first to be baptized, the native nobility "usually spoke and wrote Castilian, adopted Spanish fashion, often lived in colonial cities, sometimes married into prominent Creole families, and were well versed in the ways of colonial law and administration" (Taylor 21-2).[13] These Hispanicized native noblemen were not an exception but the norm. They adopted Castilian ways, but remained Mesoamerican subjects. Their liminal condition is still legible in the composition of their colonial names, first the Castilian name, then the Nahua: Don Diego de Alvarado Huanitzin, Don Cristóbal de Guzmán Cecetzin, Don Luis de Santa María Nanacacipactzin.[14] Twice in *Pretender*, Juan

---

11   These were members of indigenous elites from central Mexico who had Nahuatl as their principal language. There is evidence that in regions like Oaxaca, where the main language was—and remains to this day—Mixtec, indigenous leaders were not exclusively men, but also women called "cacicas."

12   For further reading, see Mundy and Katzew.

13   Initially, double identities were perhaps the byproduct of the profound sociopolitical changes brought forth by the Castilian colonial project. However, it remained in place by design, as the perdurance of Nahua material and political structures made governing the indigenous populations much easier for the Castilian administration.

14   These native rulers doubly confirmed their noble status in their names by incorporating the Spanish "Don" to the Nahua suffix "-tzin."

is reminded that changing his name does not change who he is (lines 1934-5; 2902-4), a situation that echoes that of indigenous nobility under Castilian rule.

Alarcón, in a sense, went through a similar experience. There is little doubt that he thought of himself as a Spaniard, and a noble one at that. His mother might have belonged to the powerful Mendoza dynasty, while his father's family name had been granted by the king in the 12th century for their aid in the war against the Muslims (King 18-21). Both in his theater and his private life, Alarcón insisted on his noble, Spanish background, but he was born in New Spain, which made him a *criollo* at a time when they were believed to be psychologically and morally inferior to their European born counterparts (Sahagún 76-7; Pagden, 102). His Spanish colleagues did not forget his foreign origins.[15] In a different play by Alarcón, entitled *Los favores del mundo*,[16] a Spanish man bearing the same last names as our playwright arrives at Madrid, by then the capital of the Castilian empire, a place so different that even the houses, or so he claims, are built the other way around. He is, in short, a foreigner among his own, much like the protagonist of our play, Juan, pretends to be Diego from Flanders among his own family.

Favores is the first play in the first volume of Alarcón's collected plays, and it opens with the scene mentioned above. This is how Alarcón wanted us to enter his theater: as strangers from within. *Pretender* is also part of this same volume. Again, for its strange plot device to work, Juan's inner circle must take the pretender at his word, which they do. The question is why, but there are no easy answers—Alarcón made sure of that. As Juan goes around Seville pretending to be Diego, he meets a character who, at least momentarily, seems capable of sending his whole charade tumbling to the ground: "I knew a Don Diego de Luján in Flanders, / and he looked nothing like you." Juan responds: "He too is my cousin, / and he wrote me today, in fact" (lines 1969-72). Invoking false relatives from the colonies to protect his fiction, Juan links Spaniards from the center and those from the periphery at a time when the latter were perceived as a lesser version of the former. A group as accepting as that surrounding Juan conjures a society where Spaniards from all latitudes are related to one another and accepted as such. Despite the excesses of its plot, *Pretender* wants us to consider a rather simple prob-

---

15   Lope de Vega praised Alarcón's work, but underscored his Mexican origin (Laurel f. 14r-v). So did Fernando de Vera y Mendoza (Fernández-Guerra 465) and the Count of Roca, under the pseudonym Fabio Franchi (Hartzenbusch xxxvii).

16   The title could be translated as "The Ways of the World," since the protagonist keeps up a Stoic stance in the face of both the good and the bad that transpires.

lem: what keeps the "other" from being "one of us" is not an essential, legible difference—it is simply us.

"WHAT SHIELD AGAINST SHILLINGS?": THE ROLE OF MONEY

A wholly connected world, a centralized global empire, a new society superposed on another— these historical processes allow us to make some contextual sense of a plot device that lacks all logic. The transformations produced around the globe by the emergence and expansion of the Castilian empire were swift and profound: one can imagine the vertigo felt by any one person trying to keep track of the rise of new identities—and the reader trying to keep up with Juan's charade feels a similar sense of disorientation.[17] In both the actual Castilian empire and the fictions of *Pretender*, what facilitated these transformations was money.

Because it was so expensive to defend its empire, Castile was constantly on the verge of insolvency, when not positively bankrupt. One solution was to put titles of nobility up for sale. For noble families proud of their name and status, the ascendancy of rich merchants and others to their rank was nothing short of an insult and a threat to their privileges. But trade with the American colonies had created immense wealth. People who became rich in the Americas, often referred to as the Indies, were known as *Indianos*, and many settled near Seville, the official port of entry for American cargo. Indianos had the financial capacity to acquire nobility through a monetary transaction, buying the right to be addressed as "Don" or "Doña." In short, their money allowed them to purchase a new identity.

The problem of money is ubiquitous in *Pretender*. Mentions of women and their purported love of all things material appear throughout. The idea that a successful prince should possess the means to finance the banishment of his enemies is presented early on in the play, as is the claim that one of the wonders of the world should be "a nobleman from Seville / who isn't a shopkeeper on the side" (lines 17-8), a satiric comment that highlights the proliferation of newly minted nobles. Juan is emboldened to move on with his absurd lies because, as he says, "there's nothing I can't solve with money" (line 304). Meanwhile, Sancho, his servant, considers betraying Juan for a few coins, illustrating the dire economic situation of Castilian commoners: "Who wouldn't double-cross for a doubloon? / Who could possibly resist money? / What shields against shillings?" (lines 1257-9).

---

17   For the diverse and intricate social composition of colonial Mexico, and the anxiety it provoked among the authorities and elites, see Katzew's *Casta Painting*.

Mentions of treason and traitors also abound, foregrounding Castile's xenophobia, now aggravated by a nascent, globalized economy. The expulsions and forced conversions of Jews and Muslims did little to assuage xenophobic fears: the proliferation of new money, and its capacity to transform traditionally fixed social categories with almost unchecked freedom, created instead an acute anxiety over covert enemies, both political and religious, both imagined and real. *Pretender*, then, suggests the costs to a society of assigning a price to everything.

At the edges of the play, money operates in puzzling ways: why does Juan require a formidably complicated hoax to spy on a woman who lives in his own house, while Leonardo needs nothing to pass for Juan and collect a significant amount of money in Peru? Granted, Juan gives Leonardo a stack of blank papers with his signature to facilitate his impersonation in Lima, but the purpose of these papers is to send letters to Don Rodrigo, Juan's father, in order to support Juan's fictions. The idea seems to be that a father can recognize the signature of his own son and tell if it is a forgery, but the fact remains that Rodrigo cannot even recognize his own son in the flesh. Yet apparently anyone with enough money could pass for a Don Juan de Castro or a Don Diego de Luján, either in Europe or the Americas, with relative ease.

If money unmoors identity, then a lack of money should afford stability. When Leonardo reappears near the end of the play, he narrates how, on his way to Peru, he fell off the ship. In other words, Leonardo never made it to Peru, nor did he collect the inheritance. A few lines after Leonardo's return to Seville, Juan is forced to own up to his lies and confess his duplicity. As order is restored, the play comes to an end.

Setting aside the extreme plot device, *Pretender* is quite the traditional play, dealing with the conflicts of youth—love and jealousy—and the identity crisis of a young man who disagrees with his father's authority. This relationship seems analogous to that between the metropole and New Spain, where fantastic wealth and royal absenteeism often made colonial settlers waver in their loyalty to the crown. The play employs these family dynamics to examine concepts that, in the face of an overabundance of wealth, were vital to controlling and developing the colonial project, like belonging and obedience, representation and authority. The problem is the destabilizing power of American wealth and the unwillingness of Castilians to recognize that the threat to their traditional way of life came not from imagined foreigners, but from within.

Bibliography

Bennett, Herman. "Writing into a Void: Representing Slavery and Freedom in the Narrative of Colonial America." *Social Text*, 93, vol. 25, no. 4, Winter 2007, pp. 67-89.

Brading, D.A. *The First America. The Spanish Monarchy, Creole Patriots, and the Liberal State, 1492-1867*. Cambridge UP, 1991.

Cline, Sarah. "The Spiritual Conquest Reexamined: Baptism and Christian Marriage in Early Sixteenth-Century Mexico." *Hispanic American Historical Review*, vol. 73, no. 3, 1993, pp. 453-480.

Elliot, John H. *Imperial Spain: 1469-1716*. Penguin, 2002.

Fernández-Guerra y Orbe, Luis. *Don Juan Ruiz de Alarcón y Mendoza*. Madrid, 1871.

Fuchs, Barbara. "Black Faces, White Hands: *La celosa de sí misma* and the Negotiation of Race." *MLN*, vol. 133, no. 2, 2018, pp. 242-256.

Hartzenbusch, Juan Eugenio. Introducción. *Comedias de don Juan Ruiz de Alarcón y Mendoza*, Madrid, 1882, pp. xiii-xlviii.

Heise, Ursula K. "Transvestism and the Stage Controversy in Spain and England, 1580-1680." *The Golden Age of Spanish Drama*, edited by Barbara Fuchs, Norton, 2018, pp. 479-490.

Horn, Rebecca. "Gender and Social Identity: Nahua Naming Patterns in Postconquest Central Mexico." *Indian Women of Early Mexico*, edited by Susan Schroeder, Stephanie Wood, and Robert Haskett, U of Oklahoma P, 1997, pp. 105-122.

Katzew, Ilona. *Casta Painting. Images of Race in Eighteenth-Century México*. Yale UP, 2004.

———, editor. *Contested Visions in the Spanish Colonial World*. LACMA / Yale UP, 2012.

King, Willard F. *Juan Ruiz de Alarcón, letrado y dramaturgo. Su mundo mexicano y español*. Translation by Antonio Alatorre, COLMEX, 1989.

Mignolo, Walter D. *The Darker Side of the Renaissance. Literacy, Territoriality, and Colonization*. 2nd ed., U of Michigan P, 2003.

Millares Carlo, Agustín. Noticia. *Obras completas de Juan Ruiz de Alarcón*, edited by Millares Carlo, 2nd ed., vol. 1, FCE, 1977, pp. 349-50.

Mundy, Barbara E. *The Death of Aztec Tenochtitlan, the Life of Mexico City*. U of Texas P, 2015.

Pagden, Anthony. "The Peopling of the New World. Ethnos, Race, and Empire in the Early-Modern World." *The Burdens of Empire. 1539 to the Present*. Cambridge UP, 2015, pp. 97-119.

Pastor, María Alba. *Crisis y recomposición social. Nueva España en el tránsito del siglo XVI al XVII*. FCE, 1999.

Peraza, Luis de. 1535-6. "Del antiquísimo origen y nobilísima fundación de la Imperial ciudad de Sevilla...," edited by Francisco Morales Padrón, *Boletín de la Real Academia Sevilla de Buenas Letras*, vol. 6, 1978, pp. 75-173.

Restall, Matthew. *Seven Myths of the Spanish Conquest*. Oxford UP, 2003. Reyes, Alfonso. "Ruiz de Alarcón." *Biblioteca Virtual Miguel de Cervantes*, www.cervantesvirtual.com/obra-visor/medallones/html/e2eff529-f6b6-4004-a965-83d1e5a222ce_7.html. Accessed Jan 18, 2022.

Robalino, Gladys. "Visión de México y sus criollos en *El semejante a sí mismo* de Juan Ruiz de Alarcón." *Bulletin of the Comediantes*, vol. 63, no. 2, 2011, pp. 27-38.

Rowell, Charles Henry. "The First Liberator of the Americas: The Editor's Notes / El primer libertador de las Américas: notas del editor." *Callaloo*, vol. 3, no. 1, 2008, pp. 1-11 / 181-192.

Ruiz de Alarcón, Juan. "El semejante a sí mismo." *Obras completas de Juan Ruiz de Alarcón*, edited by Agustín Millares Carlo, 2nd ed., vol. 1, FCE, 1977, pp. 351-435.

Sahagún, Bernardino. *Introduction and Indices. Florentine Codex. General History of the Things of New Spain*, edited and translated by Charles E. Dibble and Arthur J. O. Anderson, School of American Research / U of Utah P, 1982.

Seijas, Tatiana. *Asian Slaves in Colonial Mexico*. Cambridge UP, 2014. Taylor, William. Introduction. *Contested Visions in the Spanish Colonial World*, edited by Ilona Katzew, LACMA / Yale UP, 2012, pp. 15-27.

Townsend, Camilla. *Fifth Sun: A New History of the Aztecs*. Oxford UP, 2019.

Van Deusen, Nancy E. *Global Indios: The Indigenous Struggle for Justice in Sixteenth-Century Spain*. Duke UP, 2015.

Vega y Carpio, Lope Félix de. *Laurel de Apolo, con otras rimas*. Madrid, 1630.

———. "The New Art of Writing Plays." *The Golden Age of Spanish Drama*, edited by Barbara Fuchs, translated by Marvin Carlson, Norton, 2018, pp. 377-386.

Pronunciation Guide

Each vowel in Spanish has just one sound. They are pronounced as follows:

a – AH
e – EH
i – EE
o – OH
u – OO

The <u>un</u>derlined <u>sy</u>llable in each word is the <u>ac</u>cented one.

CELIO: <u>Seh</u>-lee-oh

SANCHO: <u>Sahn</u>-choh

JUAN: <u>Hwan</u>

DIEGO: Dee-<u>eh</u>-goh

ANA: <u>Ah</u>-nah

INÉS: Een-<u>ehs</u>

RODRIGO: Roh-<u>dree</u>-goh

GUILLÉN: Gee-<u>yehn</u> (as in "geese")

LEONARDO: Leh-oh-<u>nahr</u> doh

GERARDO: Hehr-<u>ahr</u>-doh

JULIA: <u>Hoo</u>-lee-ah

Characters:

CELIO, brother to Julia
Don RODRIGO, old man
SANCHO, servant and *gracioso*
GUILLÉN, squire
Don JUAN de Castro, a gentleman
LEONARDO, a gentleman
Don DIEGO de Luján, a gentleman
GERARDO, a gentleman
Doña ANA, a lady
JULIA, a lady
INÉS, servant to Doña Ana

The Pretender, or
A Man Beside Himself [1]

ACT I

SCENE 1

A room in RODRIGO's *house*

Enter JUAN, LEONARDO *and* SANCHO

JUAN	What a fine day!
LEONARDO	There's nothing like springtime in Seville.
JUAN	This city is truly the eighth wonder of the world.
LEONARDO	The list keeps getting longer, you know. There were seven once. How many are there now?
JUAN	The Escorial should be at the top of the list.
SANCHO	I know of seven new wonders far more deserving of that name.

---

1   Text based on the editions of Vern Williamsen and J. T. Abraham, "El semejante a sí mismo." *AHCT*, 1998, http//www.comedias.org/alarcon/semesi.html; and Agustín Millares Carlo, *Obras Obras completas de Juan Ruiz de Alarcón*, vol. I, FCE, 1957.

JUAN   Let's hear them,   10

SANCHO   I'll tell you.
              The first one is worth three
              of the ancient ones.

LEONARDO   What is it?

SANCHO   A woman who asks for nothing.

JUAN   Especially if she's from Madrid.

SANCHO   The second is a nobleman from Seville
              who isn't a shopkeeper on the side.
              The third's a man who's happy to be bald
              And does not comb his hair   20
              from his nape to his nose.
              The fourth, a silly young thing
              with no taste for marriage.
              The fifth, an ugly woman
              who does not lie about her age.
              The sixth, a soldier who doesn't gripe about pay
              and the seventh, a widower
              who mourns his wife.
              The eighth is an honest merchant,
              a barber's apprentice with no guitar to strum,   30
              a lady who only uses water on her face,
              a newlywed who gets along with his in-laws,
              a village church without its Peter and Paul,
              and a gambler who doesn't cry out
              "Devil take me!" from time to time...

JUAN   That's enough. The list just keeps growing.

LEONARDO   But wait—there's one more!
              Let me tell you of a wonder
              that outshines them all.

JUAN   I'm dying to hear about it   40
              since you praise it so.

LEONARDO   Listen:
             it's the great Mexican drain.

SANCHO   What in heavens are you talking about?

LEONARDO   The city of Mexico,
             the celebrated head of the Indian world,
             which is called New Spain, lies in a valley.
             It is surrounded by mountains
             like mighty walls.
             Every river and every stream   50
             that runs down those mountains
             flows into a lagoon
             that surrounds the city.
             In the year 1605,
             the little sea grew and grew
             until it found its way into the houses.
             Perhaps the drain that naturally
             swallows up the water
             as it flows into the lagoon
             had drunk its fill.   60
             Or perhaps it choked on such a flood.
             This happened in a Golden Age,
             when the great marquis of Salinas ruled,
             that heroic branch of the house of Velasco[2]
             and prudence personified,
             worthy of serving as viceroy three times over
             before he returned to Spain
             to preside over the Council of the Indies.
             This great ruler, a Lycurgus of New Spain,[3]
             tried to head off the rising waters   70
             that threatened to ruin the city.
             He convened the learned and the elders,
             and requested a thousand reports and plans
             from mapmakers and engineers.

---

2   *Velasco*: Luis de Velasco, the Younger, first Marquis of Salinas, served as a viceroy in New Spain just as his father had before him. He also served as viceroy in Peru.

3   *Lycurgus*: Spartan lawmaker famous for his military reforms.

Then the viceroy, in his wisdom,
ordered them to dig a mine under a mountain,
so that the waters might flow
to the opposite side and there join the proud river.
No sooner had he made up his mind
than they began their heroic labors.   80
Fifteen hundred workers toiled day and night.
In a little over three years, they finally reached the end:
a tunnel three leagues long to drain the lagoon.
Then, because the waters eroded the rock
and risked blocking the aqueduct,
it was all covered in immortal marble,
bringing eternal peace to the kingdom
and fame to its maker.

JUAN   Such a wondrous marvel
            justly deserves to be praised   90
            as the finest in the world.

SANCHO   So you're saying that low scoundrel, water,
            wanted to take over the earth?
            And where was wine when we needed it most?

LEONARDO   He was figuring out how to pay for the whole thing.
            They put two different taxes on each jug of wine,
            which yielded a hundred thousand ducats a year
            to finance that great drain.

SANCHO   Wine is far too noble to pay taxes
            for water, and anyone who says otherwise   100
            lies through their teeth.
            And all this so that the water
            can have marble-clad gutters to run through?
            Water, that infamous rebel
            who tried to overrun his fatherland?
            Water, who the very mountains
            cast from their bosom?
            Water, who slithers along the ground
            like a snake, and bows down to kiss

the foot of the vine? 110
Water, who falls from the heavens
like the devil himself,
shivers through the winter
and swelters through the summer,
so cheap it's almost given away,
at two quarters a barrel?
(Heavens, if only wine
could follow that example!)
Water, who has taken more lives,
more fortunes…? 120

JUAN Sancho, that's enough.

SANCHO And wine, what has it done
to deserve such treatment?
In the New World or the Old,
who has it ever hurt?

JUAN You're wrong, Sancho.
They mean to praise wine when they say
he paid to banish his rival.
After all, doesn't a powerful prince
pay to have anyone who angers him 130
slashed in the face, beaten, or sent into exile?
Is that not to his advantage?
The one scarred, beaten, or exiled is the loser.
The winner is the one whose money
can procure the sweetest revenge.

SANCHO Cheers to that!
That most sacred liquor
has found a great advocate in you.

JUAN You, fool, you do nothing but
raise your glass to it! 140

SANCHO Others have a thousand flaws,
and I have only this one.

JUAN And what about love?

SANCHO Let any man who does not love
cast the first stone.

JUAN And gambling? What about gambling?

SANCHO What is an honest man to do
while he waits for his master to call?
Isn't it worse to join in with those servants
who heap gossip on their masters 150
until they have no honor left?

JUAN Well, to keep mine safe,
I want you to leave now.
I need to talk to this gentleman
in private.

SANCHO You don't trust me, then?

JUAN You sound like the servant in a play,
pretending to be surprised
that I won't share important secrets with you.
Servants are only good for barnyard humor, 160
which they make up while brushing the horses.

SANCHO Hey, don't brush me off.

JUAN Away with you.

SANCHO I'm not an animal, you know,
though I may sleep in the stables.

SANCHO exits

LEONARDO We are alone now,
Don Juan, my friend,
tell me what's on your mind.

JUAN My dear friend,

are you presently in love? 170

LEONARDO Wow!
That's a tricky topic.
We are surrounded by love and misfortune,
but I, thank God, enjoy my freedom.
You know there was a time
when I was captive to Julia's charms,
but her endless disdain
killed both my hopes and my love.

JUAN Oh good.
Now I can tell you my troubles, 180
for your freedom will put an end
to my misfortune.

LEONARDO How so?

JUAN Would you undertake a voyage
for my sake?

LEONARDO Are we not friends?

JUAN It would be a long one.

LEONARDO For you, I'd go to the ends of the earth,
the scorching sands of Libya
or frozen tundras of Scythia.[4] 190

JUAN Actually, you'd only be going to Peru.

LEONARDO That's just around the corner.
But surely you're coming with me,
right, Don Juan?

JUAN No, you must go without me.

---

4   *Scythia*: Greco-Roman name for a distant region of Eastern Europe encompassing modern day Bulgaria, Moldova, and Ukraine.

LEONARDO   I hate the thought of not seeing you,
            but I am happy to serve you.
            Give me your arms.

JUAN   And my soul.

LEONARDO   God be with you.   200

                    LEONARDO *makes as if to leave*

JUAN   Wait, where are you going?

LEONARDO   You've asked me to go Peru
            and yet you wonder where I'm going?
            To find a ship!

JUAN   Stop.

LEONARDO   This is how a true friend must act.

JUAN   I knew you'd do me this great favor,
            but would you really board the ship
            without even knowing why
            or to what end?   210

LEONARDO   It is enough to know it pleases you.
            What else does one need to know
            when ordered to leave?
            It's not my place to question
            such a worthy cause.
            I thought you just wanted me to go,
            so I was setting off, straight to Peru.

JUAN   God keep you.
            I know such a long journey
            must seem strange to you.   220
            Believe me, if I could put my trust in anyone else,
            I'd never ask this of such a dear friend.

LEONARDO   What must I do?

JUAN   Allow me to explain.

LEONARDO   Of course.

JUAN   You know my uncle's life was cut short by the Fates.[5]
            He left a daughter, Ana, whom I would die for.
            My father became guardian to this girl
            (not that such an angel needs one)
            and now treats me like a cruel stepfather.   230
            He brought her into our home,
            the better to watch over her
            But you shouldn't keep your gunpowder
            near the fire.
            So beautiful and charming was she,
            that after a few exchanges,
            Cupid quickly set my heart ablaze.[6]
            Soon I found myself under his sway.
            That blind god is a tyrant.
            It's no wonder a philosopher   240
            painted Love with roses in one hand
            and thorns in the other.
            And now my father, my cruel enemy,
            is sending me across the sea to Lima
            to claim a certain inheritance.
            Either he is aware of our love
            and would not have her be my wife
            because he hopes for a more appropriate match,
            or his own desires, which burn all the hotter
            in an old man's cold blood,   250
            make him send me away.
            At this, I find my soul in such a state
            that my life... my...
            only one who has truly loved
            could ever understand.
            But Cupid has wings,

---

5   *Fates*: Greco-Roman incarnations of destiny.
6   *Cupid:* Roman God of love.

for lovers' wits take flight
when they are in his thrall.
I produce a thousand schemes a minute
and finally light on one that will grant me   260
the fame of the treacherous Sinon[7]
and an end to my torment.
I will live with my father and my lady Ana,
without being recognized by either.
What won't a lover attempt?
I have another cousin in Madrid,
Don Diego de Luján is his name,
who's finally back from the wars in Flanders
after a long absence.
I've written to him about the sad state of my affairs.   270
And he, more a friend than just a relative,
has said he'll give his life for my sake.
So I've written him again
and outlined the scheme
by which I hope to realize my purpose.
And so that you may know as well,
the plan is this:
my cousin Diego and I will spread the word
that we look remarkably alike.
I've told him to write my father,   280
feigning a desire to come to Seville
to see this resemblance for himself before I leave,
so that all who know us both
can marvel at our common likeness.
And that's not all: we have another plan.
Don Diego sent my father a portrait of me
as if it were his likeness—I had sent it to him first.
And I did the same with his father—
that is, with my uncle, sending him a letter
along with a portrait of my cousin   290
that I claimed to be me.
So, with my plot set in motion,
I happily pretend to prepare for my trip.

---

7   *Sinon*: A Greek soldier in the Trojan war, known for his eloquence in tricking the Trojans.

That, too, is part of the plan.
I have everything one might want on board,
and I have arranged for all the meals.
It's all so fine it almost makes me want to sail away.
You and I will embark on this journey together.
At Cadiz, we'll bid farewell to Sancho,
my friends, and my family.   300
The winged vessel will take off for all to see,
lest anyone think I've remained ashore.
But I'll pay for another boat to bring me back.
There's nothing I can't solve with money.
I will secretly return to await
my cousin Diego's arrival next month.
He has agreed to act as my servant
while I pretend to be him
in front of my father and my beloved.
You, dear Leonardo, will travel to Lima,   310
where you will take my name,
since no one knows you there.
I'll give you papers.
I'm amused at the very thought
of you becoming me.
I mean, you're basically my brother already,
you're such a good friend.
There you will claim that inheritance for me,
and since my presence here
will make my father suspicious,   320
I'll give you some papers
with my signature on them[8]
so you can send letters home
to allay his suspicions.
And I, meanwhile, will conquer
the cause of all my sorrows,
as long as that blind deity
does not neglect a heart
that's been spurred to such designs
by his poisoned arrow.   330

---

8   Nobles often had their secretaries write letters on their behalf, which were marked with personal signatures or rubrics to attest to their origins, like signing a blank check today.

LEONARDO   So you mean to say, Don Juan,
            that you've faked a resemblance
            to your cousin, Don Diego de Luján,
            by having him send your father
            your portrait instead of his own,
            so you can stay here?

JUAN   Yes, and I've done the same to his father:
            I've sent a portrait of Don Diego,
            his son and my cousin, in place of my own.

LEONARDO   But has your uncle never met you?   340

JUAN   My uncle has never seen me,
            nor has my father ever seen my cousin.

LEONARDO   There is no man alive
            who can match your singular wit.
            But tell me, why deceive your beloved
            and not let her in on the secret?

JUAN   My cousin Ana has shown me constant love,
            yet I fear she might be deceiving me.
            And so I will become Don Diego
            and court her in that disguise   350
            to test if her love is true.

LEONARDO   In that case, wouldn't it be a better idea
            to have someone else woo her?

JUAN   That would be impertinent.[9]
            She could fall for the other man,
            and to test her in that way is to lose her.

---

9   *Impertinent*: references the general ill-advisedness of love tests for their
tendency to backfire, as in the "Tale of Impertinent Curiosity" in the first part *Don
Quijote*, in which Anselmo, dogged by curiosity over the faithfulness of his wife Ca-
mila, asks his friend Lotario to try to seduce her. While she initially refuses, the two
eventually become lovers precisely due to Anselmo's insistence that Lotario test Ca-
mila's love, and Anselmo dies of heartbreak.

But this way, if she takes me for myself
then it all stays in the family.
If she falls for me as Don Diego,
I alone will know what she's capable of   360
without her knowing another man.

LEONARDO   But why do you want
             Don Diego in the middle?

JUAN   In order to properly fool his father and mine,
             and so my plot will work even better.
             And in Don Diego I'll gain a faithful friend
             to confide in.

LEONARDO   Well, that makes perfect sense.

JUAN   I've sent him a letter of credit
             for a hundred doubloons   370
             to cover expenses.

LEONARDO   That's always your way of getting
             what you want.

JUAN   Well, I'm rich,
             so why should I spare any expense
             to solve my problems?
             Spending freely always leads to victory.

LEONARDO   And your victory will be well-deserved.

JUAN   Certainly, if you help me.

LEONARDO   Well then,   380
             I'll prepare for my voyage.

JUAN   You'll have two thousand *escudos*
             for the expenses.

LEONARDO   There's no need.

JUAN   I would not ordinarily do as much,
although even this is too little,
but my father has given me
generous credit for Lima,
and you shall have it,
so that you may be at ease   390
until you can collect the inheritance.

LEONARDO   I shouldn't, I shouldn't,
and yet I am much obliged.

JUAN   On the contrary,
giving my life is but little
for one who gives life to my hopes.

LEONARDO *exits*

JUAN   Increase in prosperous fortune,
and for the unhappy, ease,
to this natural secret, the master key:
knowing two wills will enclose soon   400
one; of human rule the platoon,
the column, anchor on the unsure seas
of mortal life; keeping peace
over everything under the moon—
this is sacred friendship, divine
virtue not delaying its tender gifts,
friendship itself the fruit
to which men naturally incline
so that he who without it lives,
lives like a beast, like a brute.   410

SCENE 2

Enter SANCHO

SANCHO   Are you done telling secrets?

JUAN   What's it to you, Sancho?

SANCHO   (*Aside*) He's sure been acting strange
now that he's headed for Peru
Since they announced his journey to Lima,
he's no longer to my taste,
not with sugar, not with lime.
(*To* JUAN) Have you lost faith in old Sancho?

JUAN   Oh, Sancho, stop whining.

SANCHO   But what would we do without wine?   420

JUAN   You and your obsessions!

SANCHO   And you with yours.
You're always going on
about your beloved cousin.

JUAN   She consumes me.
Wait! Here she comes.
Heavens, is that a love letter
she's reading?

Enter ANA *reading a letter, without seeing* JUAN *and* SANCHO

SANCHO   (*Aside*) Looks like he's real upset.
All it takes is a spark of suspicion   430
to light a powder keg of jealousy.

JUAN   (*Aside to* SANCHO) I will either kill her or kill myself.

SANCHO   You look like you're about to go off.
Tell me, sir: which is worse,
getting drunk or going crazy?

JUAN   Damn you, you scoundrel!

JUAN *strikes* SANCHO

SANCHO   By God, you knocked a tooth out!

JUAN *takes the letter from* ANA

JUAN   Let go, you faithless...

ANA   Stop, cousin! Must we always
                be at each other for no reason?   440
                This behavior does not endear you to me.

SANCHO   (*Aside*) He pursues her like a feral cat,
                biting and clawing to get his way.
                He once had a gentler side,
                but now that he's off to Peru,
                he's so desperate that he seems
                like he's on his way to hell.

                        JUAN *reads the letter*

ANA   It's a letter from your cousin Diego at court.

JUAN   Oh, how nice.
                So my cousin knows you   450
                and cares to write to you?

ANA   Look here, you fool,
                it's addressed to your father.

JUAN   Oh, I see.

ANA   God knows I committed
                no crime in reading it!
                Don Juan, a suspicious mind
                will see signs everywhere.
                But know that it is wrong
                to scold without just cause.   460

JUAN   Why must you read
                what another man has written?

ANA   I saw it on the desk,
                It was open, and I'm a woman.
                Must you scold me for this, too?

JUAN   Did you fall for his style?

ANA   You're certainly pig-headed today,
              Don Juan, or just out of your mind.

JUAN   Once I leave,
              my place in your heart will be open—   470
              that is why you go rummaging through papers,
              to see who might deserve it.

ANA   And just glancing at a letter will do that?

JUAN   Doña Ana, it doesn't take much
              for a woman to fall in love.

SANCHO   While we're on this topic,
              and so that the two of you
              will give it a break, my lord and lady,
              I'd like to tell you a true story
              from when I was young.   480
              I had a certain Juan Lobo for a friend.[10]
              I brought him along once
              to see a certain girl of mine.
              He stood quietly while I spoke
              some words to my love—
              you know how the story goes.
              Now and then, my girl would eye
              this Lobo, observing how loyally
              he waited for me.
              And then she fell in love with him,   490
              just because he never made a move,
              while I carried on and on.

JUAN   Sancho, the slightest sign is enough
              to condemn the unfortunate.

ANA   You're always complaining

---

10   *Lobo:* Spanish for wolf.

for no reason, Don Juan.
I confess, cousin, that I read
the letter with pleasure.
And what is more,
I esteem its author   500
because he looks like you.
He says God made you two so alike
that it tricks your friends,
all of whom take him for you.

JUAN   (*Aside*) Everything proceeds according to plan.
            (*Aloud*) He is my cousin.
            It is not so strange that we look alike.

SANCHO   Two men who resemble each other
            is no stranger than
            two suits to be identical   510
            when cut from the same cloth.

JUAN   But if someone should behold
            my cousin in my presence,
            I have no doubt that they
            would find us very different.
            And now that the heavens
            have decreed that
            I should leave you,
            I want to give you
            this portrait of myself.   520
            Don Diego writes that
            he will come to see me
            as soon as possible,
            yet my ship is about to sail.
            I have asked my father
            —if only he would listen—
            to host him and care for him
            as he would for me.
            I want to ask the same of you,
            because if you treat him well   530
            in remembrance of me,

your love for me will only grow.
As long, of course,
as you remain careful and modest.
Otherwise, the portrait may
take the place of the original.
So that Don Diego's fire
may never spark love in you,
you must always speak as if to Don Juan,
even if it is Don Diego who speaks to you.   540
Thus, while I don't see you,
forget your troubles
by gazing on this portrait.
Let yourself be deceived
by your desire.

ANA   Oh God! How can I bear to hear
these instructions for your absence,
Don Juan, without breaking into tears?

JUAN   Are you crying?

ANA   Ask me if I can live while you're away.   550

JUAN   I confess that I did not expect
such feeling from your cold heart.
Do not cry, my lady,
unless by doing so
you would make my departure glad,
having confirmed my good fortune.
Do not shed those pearly tears
on those roses,
or the dawn, in its haste
to collect them all,   560
will make the sun rise sooner,
making the day run faster,
and bring my happiness
to a swifter end.
Don't shed all your tears today.
Save some for when I'm gone.

Don't let your fears
torment you too soon.
As you can see, I am still here.
Save some sorrow for my absence, 570
for if your fever breaks too soon,
you might be too quickly cured.

ANA   May God punish me, my love,
if I find solace in your absence.
May I be despised by any future husband!
May God...!

SANCHO   Enough "mays."
My lord, here comes the old man.

JUAN   Time will tell whether
those fine feelings you allege 580
are true.

ANA and JUAN *exit*

SANCHO   "May God" this and "may God" that!
Lovers! I tell you, they call on God
more than the dying.

Enter INÉS

INÉS   How's Don Juan?

SANCHO   That's a good one!
What am I, Inés, the joker?
Why do you ask for the jack,
with so much riding on the ace?

INÉS   Who is the jack? 590

SANCHO   Don Juan.

INÉS   And the ace?

SANCHO   That's me, because I'm always ahead.
          But tell me, how are you faring
          now that you know I'm leaving?

INÉS   You're leaving?
SANCHO   For Pete's sake!
          Had you forgotten, Inés?
          A sign of true devotion.

INÉS   Are you actually going to Peru?   600

SANCHO   (*Aside*) There goes Troy.[11]
          (*Aloud*) Yes, I am.

INÉS   What will you send me from abroad?

SANCHO   I will send you the devil!
          Behold the sorrow with which
          this sad news is received!
          Note how she girds herself
          to face the approaching pain!
          Such is the infamous tyranny of women:
          "I am coming" has the ring of "give me something,"   610
          and "I am going" echoes back "send me something."
          Is there no "welcome" to "I'm home,"
          no "come back soon" to "I am going"?
          A masked bandit—that is how Love
          should be painted.
          I barely glimpsed the woman,
          and now I must pay up?
          It's a terrible gamble, having to pay
          before she shows her hand.
          "Her hand," I say? Even less.   620
          Try courting a veiled woman—
          she'll be asking for ribbons and gloves
          before you see a thing.
          "What will you send me?" That's nice!

---

11   *"There goes Troy"*: Spanish saying indicating that some venture has failed or
ended disastrously, or is about to end that way, akin to "the jig is up."

The firmest love lasts but a day.
If she would only say "bring me"
which is like saying "come back!"
But "send me" only means "stay there."
Damned be the fool who trusts in them,
who sends or brings or gives them gifts!   630
Who could bear it! There is nothing for it
but to hold your purse close
and give her an earful!

SANCHO *exits*

INÉS   Wait, Sancho, look, I'm crying.
I'm not asking for anything,
if my asking makes you angry,
I wanted to soften the blow
of your leaving for the Indies
by imagining the riches
I expected from your hands.   640
"Who could bear it?" you say,
but you are more the fool.
You hold onto your purse,
yet expect me to be true!

INÉS *exits*

SCENE 3

Room in CELIO's *house Enter* LEONARDO *and* GUILLÉN

GUILLÉN   Wait here, Leonardo,
while I inform my lady
of your visit.

GUILLÉN *exits*

LEONARDO   For Julia to call me now?
I am beside myself.

I haven't seen her in a thousand days,   650
since she has never been willing.
The embers of love grow cold
from such long absence,
yet now she remembers me?
When I'm about to leave,
she wants to rekindle my affections
with a fond farewell?
But she does not call me for love's sake—
would that I were so fortunate.
She must know that I'm on my way to the Indies   660
and wants to ask me for something.
But here she comes.
The very sound of her footsteps undoes me—
my blood freezes in my veins
while my heart is set ablaze.
How easy it is to rekindle old fires.
Indeed, true love dies hard.

Enter JULIA

JULIA   Leonardo, my lord,
was it not time for us to meet again?

LEONARDO   You should be the one to answer that.   670

JULIA   I did—and my answer was to call you.

LEONARDO   And mine was to come here
at your request, if only to show
you that your word is my command.

JULIA   They say you're going to the Indies.

LEONARDO   That is so, unless you order me to stay.

JULIA   If an order is all it takes,
then I order you to not go away.
Forgive me for being so blunt—

               I am taking you at your word.   680

LEONARDO   Unless I'm missing something,
             you wish to impose on me
             a new kind of cruelty,
             one that passes for a favor.

JULIA   What do you mean?

LEONARDO   I'll speak frankly, for I'm about to leave.
             After so much disdain,
             you only order me to stay because
             if I go, you'll have no one
             on whom to inflict your cruelties.   690
             But no more, Julia.
             I freed my neck from your yoke once before,
             and I'm now at liberty to wring out
             the garments that were once
             drenched in the sea of Love.
             No more suffering only to please you.
             No more risking my life
             for your fickle whims.
             You fled when I pursued you—
             and now that I flee, you pursue me.   700
             What you feel now, Julia,
             is what I felt before.
             But today I claim a major victory
             with my absence, as I wrest
             this body from your cruelty,
             this soul from your memory.

JULIA   I swear you scold with such passion!
             You now imagine yourself avenged,
             but you're a fool who has thrown
             all strength into the void.   710
             Who said that my plea
             that you not leave was because
             I love you and your leaving brings me pain?
             My cousin Leonor likes you well, and

asked me, because you once loved me so much—
if that was even true—to request that you stay.
For my part, the greater favor
would be for you to leave.

LEONARDO   That's enough. It's ridiculous
to indulge your disdain now,   720
and since I no longer love you,
you are also missing the mark.
Don't think that my wayward arrow
weighs on me, for at least
we exchanged a few shots.
Since I have let you know
what I mean to do,
therein lies my revenge.
My intentions were enough to offend you,
even more than my clumsy attempts.   730
If only I could find a way to stay!
Just to make you sorry,
God knows I would stay.

JULIA   At least you approve of my harshness.
How wrong it would be for me to love
someone as low as you, so set on revenge.

LEONARDO   Don't attribute my disobedience
to vengeance, as God knows
that it was only born of mistrust.
I thought that seeing me leave   740
would awaken your love,
and it was your harshness I feared
if I continued to pursue you.
Otherwise, what greater glory,
what richer Indies could I find,
having loved you so long,
than to triumph over your disdain?
Love does not so easily
lay down its arms.

JULIA   It seems to me, sir, that you   750
             are beginning to turn back the page.

LEONARDO   To deny how long I've loved you
             is to deny the sea has waves.

JULIA   Leonardo, is there any greater denial
             than to deny what I ask of you?

LEONARDO   That was not denial, but fear
             of how harsh you've been to me.

JULIA   Does love never change,
             Leonardo? Am I not a woman?

LEONARDO   My Julia, what would I not do   760
             to see such change in you?

JULIA   Then do what I say, and trust
             that I am done with disdain.

LEONARDO   What are you saying?

JULIA   Just what you heard.
             I am persuaded by your words,
             and you must trust mine.

LEONARDO   How cruel! What has moved you
             now to feign this change of heart?

JULIA   If I have not told you the truth,   770
             let there be no pity for my love
             and no hope for my desire.

LEONARDO   When by all rights
             I should have softened your heart,
             my lady, I never could.
             Why am I to think
             you have softened for me now,

with no reason?

JULIA   Oh, Leonardo, how little you understand
               what women are like.   780
               Is it not enough to know
               that you plan to leave me?
               When you were my prisoner,
               Love was asleep on its watch.
               Yet it awoke at the first sign
               of the prisoner's escape.
               I don't know what change
               came over me in an instant,
               but with it, I burned
               and froze all at once.   790
               My confidence in your love
               was ash over my fire,
               and the change in you
               was like a breath of wind
               that discovered the live embers beneath.
               Don't punish me now
               because my love denied you,
               as I too have ignored
               how much my heart adores you.
               It is your absence that shows   800
               how much I delight in your presence.
               Why must I learn such lessons
               from one who kills me?
               Don't ruin your hopes
               by punishing my severity,
               for vengeance is madness
               if it kills the one who seeks revenge.
               Now you're quiet? What can I hope for?
               To take so long in responding
               is as good as turning me down.   810
               How can you do this to me?
               Say something! What are you waiting for?

LEONARDO   Oh, my Julia!

JULIA	What's wrong? If you don't believe what I say, I will show.
LEONARDO	You don't understand.
JULIA	So tell me!
LEONARDO	Cruel love always mixes pleasure with pain. I've given Don Juan de Castro my word 820 to go with him to Peru, and so I must, even if it costs me my life. It is as good as lost, since I must part from you.
JULIA	My pleas to Don Juan will release you from your word.
LEONARDO	Do not attempt such madness. He'll think it's a ploy and that I've changed my mind.

Enter JUAN

JUAN	Ah, you must be eager to go, Leonardo, 830 since you've come to ask Julia for her blessing.
JULIA	And you, who take him from me, must be here as my curse.
JUAN	You can have Leonardo, Julia, if that's what you want.
JULIA	Yes, that is what I want.
JUAN	Your word is my command.
LEONARDO	Julia, you should know this offends me Don Juan, I do not understand this. What kind of friend do you take me for? 840

JUAN　　　　I cannot ask this of you
if it makes you so unhappy.

LEONARDO　　God forbid that love
should overcome friendship.

JUAN　　　　It runs both ways:
if friendship leads you
to trample your own good,
then that same friendship in me
won't allow it, and so
your love must triumph.　　　　850

LEONARDO　　I must keep my word.
I know how much you need me,
Don Juan.

JUAN　　　　Leonardo, I can find someone
to go in your place.

LEONARDO　　It's too late, you won't find
anyone now.

JULIA　　　　Now that Don Juan has released you,
don't claim you have an obligation to him
or deny that you are set on vengeance.　　　　860
Take your revenge. Leave, oh my enemy,
for I...

LEONARDO　　Listen, Julia, dearest,
if I don't leave my life here with you,
let the sea swallow me whole.
If not...

JULIA　　　　Set the oaths aside, Leonardo.
It's actions I believe in.

LEONARDO　　I want nothing more than to please you.

JUAN   You have given Julia good reason to complain.   870

LEONARDO   You should not push me to do
                what is not right.

JUAN   What Julia wants is what's right.

LEONARDO   My obligation is what's right.

JUAN   Don Juan waives his claim.

LEONARDO   That's true, but in this tight predicament,
                what he has done for courtesy
                does not release me from my obligation.

JULIA   You play me false!

                        Enter GUILLÉN

GUILLÉN   Lady, your brother.   880

JULIA   Don Juan, I beg of you.

JUAN   Heaven couldn't grant you a better advocate.

                        Enter CELIO *and* GERARDO

CELIO   Gentlemen! You, in this house?

JUAN   We have both come to bid you farewell.

JULIA   Don Juan is on his way to the Indies
                and has come to bid farewell
                as any nobleman might.

CELIO   And Leonardo?

JULIA   I assume he's going as far as Cadiz with him.

Leonardo	And from Cadiz to Lima.	890
Julia	(*Aside*) Again he plays me false!	
Celio	I wish you good fortune on your journey.	
Juan	Thank you. Julia, I hope to hear the happy news that you have married one who deserves you.	
Julia	Goodbye.	
Leonardo	Goodbye, Celio.	
Celio	Goodbye, Leonardo.	
Leonardo	Julia, may God grant that I see you, as my heart desires.	900
Julia	God be with you.	
Gerardo	(*Aside*) I burn with jealousy.	
Julia	(*Aside*) Take my life, oh heavens!	

Julia and Gerardo speak aside

Gerardo	Listen to me, faithless Julia.
Julia	(*Aside*) Just what I need now. (*Aloud*) Let go of me!
Gerardo	Listen!
Julia	I can't stand it!

Julia exits

GERARDO   I can't bear it!   910

              CELIO, GERARDO, *and* GUILLÉN *exit*

JUAN   Now that we're alone,
              you can declare your intentions.

LEONARDO   The one who loves me when I'm gone
              will not love me if I stay.

JUAN   Do you care for her?

LEONARDO   My soul adores her beauty once again.

JUAN   Stay here to enjoy it.

LEONARDO   Must you start this again?
              I will go, by God,
              for that will test   920
              her devotion to me
              and prove my friendship to you.

ACT II

SCENE 1

Enter RODRIGO, ANA *and* INÉS, *with* SANCHO *in traveling clothes*

SANCHO My lord, Leonardo and I
all left here on a Monday,
and arrived in Cadiz on Thursday,
just as the sun tucked itself in.
Don Fernando was our host,
that branch of your noble house
who is as generous as they say,
offering fine gifts and largesse. 930
On Saturday, as the last relics of darkness
were fleeing from the dawn,
and in the east, peaks shone ruby and gold,
the flagship set off a cannon,
whose fire shot out amid smoke and sparks,
as though among clouds and lightning.
"Raise anchor!" all shouted in reply.
All hurried to embark,
and at once, the sandy riverbank
was full of crowds. 940
We too gathered there to mount
those steeds of the sea
who raced through waters with oars.
We boarded the galleon.
I set eyes and ears
on tasks and chants

no novice could understand.
I was there until 10 o'clock
speaking with my master,
as he entrusted me with all those things   950
a man his age is concerned with.
Then the cannon went off again,
and my master dismissed me,
so I was obliged to leave the ship,
and return to shore.
Its thunder had hardly split the air
when the flagship raised its sails
and the winds made light of the hefty load.
On the stern, Don Lope, that heroic general,
scion of the Díez, the Aux and the Armendárez,   960
the cross of Calatrava on his breast,[12]
judged by all for his deeds and habits
as worthy of a greater charge
from our saintly king, for so often
has he secured the unquiet seas
and has made them pay their tribute
to Spain in entire fleets of silver.
And so the flagship sailed off,
blocking out the sun
in a flurry of smoke   970
from cannons and muskets.
Behind her sailed your son's ship,
pulling up her anchors alongside
and unfurling its sails,
crashing through the crystalline blue.
My lord stood at the railing,
and I watched as, bit by bit,
he departed from the Andalusian shores.
My tears got in the way,
yet my loyalty would not   980

---

12   *Cross of Calatrava*: The Order of Calatrava was one of three major Spanish religious-military orders, originally founded to counter Muslim forces in the 12th
century. These orders became very powerful, and owned immense estates, towns and
fortresses.

allow me to look away.
I followed with my eye as far as I could,
until distance made everything
blend into confusion,
and each ship seemed nothing
but the tiny relic of a cloud.
With this sight, I returned to the inn
and prepared my own journey,
leaving Cadiz that same day at twilight.
I slept in Sanlucar, and discovered, 990
to my misfortune, that on Monday
there would be a bullfight
for the duke's particular pleasure,
and I stayed there to watch it.
The bulls arrived Monday
and I, like any good sightseer,
wandered around the entire plaza.
Some she-devil put the evil eye on me,
for as I stood waiting for the first bull,
I was chased, and before I could hide 1000
I was grabbed by this here buttock
and given such a shake
that the horn wounded me
and the blow stunned me.
When I came to,
from the near ecstasy in which I lay,
I found myself with one more hole
than usual in the back,
unfastened and penniless,
for those who assist in these cases 1010
first go for the wallet
and then tend to any injuries.
Three weeks I have spent
in waiting for my wound to heal,
and that's why I'm so late, sir,
with this news and these letters.

RODRIGO *takes the letters and* ANA *cries*

RODRIGO　　May God keep him.

SANCHO　　(*Aside to* ANA) Much though your love may weep,
my lord has wept a thousand tears
for each one of yours.　　　　　　　　　　　　1020

ANA　　What did he tell you?

SANCHO　　Well...
One who departs when he's so in love...
He charged me with your care
a million times and more.
When we mounted and dismounted,
on the road and at the inn,
as we ate and as we paid,
on the river and the sea,
by night and by day,　　　　　　　　　　　　1030
and as every last prayer
reached its final "Amen,"
it was "Watch over Ana!
That's why you must stay
in Spain, Sancho," he told me.
And the truth is I don't mind:
I don't much like the sea.

ANA *cries*

SANCHO　　(*To* INÉS) While Don Rodrigo reads
and Doña Ana cries,
let's you and me talk, you tyrant.　　　　　　1040
Tell me, where do I stand with you?
Have you given your word to some other,
luckier man than me?
Two years as your suitor
only got me pinched all over.
Speak. Don't be rude,
even if you must be coy.

INÉS　　Didn't you claim

you were leaving for the Indies?

SANCHO   What better Indies than Inés?   1050
          To show you what a foolish idea
          it was to leave for the Indies
          I will ask a poet
          to paint your beauty.
          Your hair will be gold,
          your forehead silver,
          your teeth pearls,
          your lips coral.
          And so, you see,
          if your beauty itself   1060
          is the measure of all wealth,
          then what better Indies
          can there be than Inés?

SCENE 2

Enter JUAN, *in completely different dress, and* DIEGO, *dressed for travel*

JUAN   I am at your feet, sir.

RODRIGO   Is that Juan?

ANA   Is that my Juan,
          or Don Diego de Luján,
          who is the very image of him?

JUAN   I am Don Juan.

SANCHO   Holy heavens!   1070
          Don Juan? How can it be?
          I myself watched him disappear
          from view on the salty seas.

JUAN   And is it such a miracle if I return?

RODRIGO   If that were the case,
the news would have reached us
long before you got to Seville.

JUAN   The galleon was so smashed
and broken that we made it to Lisbon alive
only because God was our captain.   1080
I felt it was impossible
to embark once again, and so
I took the road post-haste
and got here before news of my departure.

RODRIGO   Embrace me, son. Good God,
what danger you have escaped!

ANA   Beloved cousin, I'm glad you are well.

JUAN   Dear cousin!

ANA   Is it really you

SANCHO   (*Aside to* INÉS) It's his face and voice,   1090
Inés, but I don't recognize those clothes
or his beard, or anything else.
Don Juan's beard is not so full.
If it's really Don Diego de Luján
pretending to be Don Juan,
they'll soon fish it out of him.
(*To* JUAN) Give me your arms,
and let Philandro welcome you.

JUAN   My Philandro!

SANCHO   Me, Philandro! Oh, that's good!   1100
By God, I caught him out!
I am Armindo.

JUAN   I let you lead me astray,
Armindo, just to bait you.

SANCHO   Oh, that's nice!
                Armindo? He fell for it again.
                By my life, that is not Don Juan!
DIEGO   You've discovered his trick.

JUAN   Forgive Don Diego de Luján
                for baiting you in this way.   1110

RODRIGO   What are you saying?

JUAN   I wanted to see
                if the resemblance between
                Don Juan and myself
                was as strong as people claim.
                Having fooled his father,
                I see that I am exactly like him.

RODRIGO   Well, I don't much appreciate
                being baited. You went too far.
                Yet I still have my doubts whether   1120
                you're Don Diego or Don Juan.

JUAN   (*As he hands over the letters*) These letters of introduction
                will confirm it.

RODRIGO   In truth, if I remember correctly,
                in that little portrait you sent me[13]
                you were wearing those same clothes.

                         RODRIGO *reads*

JUAN   That's true!

ANA   (*Aside*) What will I do now?

SANCHO   Who could have known?
                Now that I've looked him over,   1130

---

13   A *retratillo*, or portrait miniature, was a common item exchanged between
family members, loved ones, or potential spouses.

I spot a thousand differences
(*Aside to* INÉS) Can't you see it, Inés?
Don't you see how this one hunches over,
and is a little thinner,
and his feet are bigger?
I laugh to think how we fell for it.
He doesn't match up at all.
Look closely. This one looks like a Jew.
And the servant! Is he not ugly, Inés?
Next to him, I am Narcissus!   1140
By God, if the master is a Jew,[14]
the servant is a Pharisee.

INÉS   Sancho, you're not seeing straight.
              The servant looks very dapper.

SANCHO   Sure, sure! You like him?
              Then may God forgive Sancho. Amen.

RODRIGO   You are welcome, Don Diego de Luján,
              and you ease our sorrow
              over Juan's absence.
              You so resemble him   1150
              that I see the very image of him in you.
              And so I hope that you will
              stay for a long time here in Seville.
              We will host Don Diego
              in my son's room.
              Niece, I beg you to treat him
              as Juan has requested.
              Now, come in and rest, Diego.
              God save me! In my life
              I've never seen such a likeness.   1160

RODRIGO *and* INÉS *exit*

---

14   Jews were persecuted and ultimately expelled from Spain in 1492. Sancho's
comment reflects Catholic anxiety about cryptojudaism—individuals who pretended to have converted to Catholicism while continuing to practice Judaism in secret.

JUAN Cousin, give me your arms.

ANA Again?

ANA *embraces* JUAN

JUAN Well, you have not yet embraced
Don Diego, have you?

SANCHO (*Aside*) What a show of resistance, by God!
Again? No hesitation, either.
(*To* ANA) You know that I must write
my lord and tell him all that you do.

ANA What do you expect?
Don Diego is his very portrait, 1170
I could not resist him.

JUAN *and* DIEGO *speak aside*

JUAN See how quickly she embraced me,
Diego! Heavens, how easy!

DIEGO Well, what are you after?
Are you jealous of yourself?

JUAN Why not? If she embraces me as Don Diego,
does she not offend me as Don Juan?

DIEGO If Don Diego de Luján is her cousin,
tell me, I beg you, why you are
so worried about a cousinly embrace? 1180

JUAN I am also her cousin,
and with me she speaks of love.

ANA Don Diego?

JUAN My dear cousin.

ANA   What is that fellow
          arguing with you about?
          (*Aside*) Good God,
          they're identical!

JUAN   The man you see before you, Ana,
          is my equal in blood and good sense—   1190
          I only surpass him in my good fortune.

SANCHO   Oh, if Inés were to hear this!

JUAN   With him I'm always an open book.
          His merits have made of him
          a companion rather than a servant.
          I told him that you outmatch your own reputation
          and he reminded me of a lady
          who might be jealous of our cousinly embrace.
          Given your perfection,
          I told him I might   1200
          leave for greener pastures.
          Judge now who is in the right.

ANA   Neither of you, it seems to me.
          Not you, for no beauty
          would excuse such fickleness.
          Nor he, who holds you back,
          for a servant should see
          to his master's pleasure
          rather than to what he owes another.

JUAN   I appeal your sentence,   1210
          for a change of heart
          should not be condemned
          when one exchanges earth for heaven.
          In heaven, the soul lies firmly in its place
          while love fervently seeks
          the greatest beauty.
          And since yours is unmatched,
          no sooner had I seen you

than I said to my love:
"Here must you reside,   1220
here shall you dwell eternally,
here must all past memories die."

Sancho   And so it begins.
            It's pretend or perish.
            (*Aside to* Ana) Don't listen to him, Doña Ana.

Ana   Leave me! What a bore!

Juan   (*Aside to* Diego) She is upset because I'm in her way.
            By God, she is fickle!

Diego   And you, jealous for no reason.

Ana   (*Aside*) I can't stop looking at him.   1230
            His face, his voice, his body
            are all those of my absent beloved.
            I can't let him out of my sight—
            just like Don Juan.
            Yet Sancho is getting suspicious,
            and I must...
            (*Aloud*) You must rest now.

Juan   My dear cousin,
            I can no longer find rest without you.

Ana   You flatter me?   1240
            (*Aside*) Good God!
            He's exactly the same!

                        Ana *exits*

Juan   Goodbye.

Sancho   (*Aside*) There's something fishy here.
            I must look sharp.

JUAN   You could hardly be any more determined
           to foil me if I were your enemy, my man.
           Tell me, what have I done to you?
           (*Aside*) I will test his loyalty.

SANCHO   All wish to serve you here,   1250
           as well they should.

JUAN   Let us be friends,
           and let these doubloons
           prove our friendship.
           So tell me: what reason do you have
           to keep my lovely cousin away from me?

SANCHO   (*Aside*) Who wouldn't double-cross for a doubloon?
           Who could possibly resist money?
           What shield against shillings?
           Gold will make a dumb man speak—   1260
           it will even make chatty barbers shut up!

                  JUAN *gives* SANCHO *a coin*

JUAN   (*Aside*) Now this defense is breached,
           for he takes the bribe.
           The honor of an absent man
           lasts only till someone attacks it.

SANCHO   If I must confess the truth,
           my lord Don Juan
           is so in love with Doña Ana
           that he is out of his mind.
           And so in his absence   1270
           he charged me, oh heavy load,
           to be his vengeful angel in this paradise,
           though I wield no sword.

JUAN   (*Aside*) See how quickly he's confessed,
           glad of the bribe!
           What might have required torture in others,
           pleasure has achieved in him.

No one cares for courtesies any longer,
nor do they lead to anything good.
The only sane thing is to do as others do.   1280
Might makes right, as the saying goes.
(*Aloud*) But I am here. Help me
in my amorous quest,
and exchange a dubious hope
for a friendship most true.
You are making her angry, too.
You shouldn't worry about losing
one absent friend, if you gain
two who are actually here.
Don Juan won't know of this offense to him.   1290
If he does find out and you lose him,
then I'll take you into my service,
and you'll be compensated for any harm.

SANCHO   By God, that sermon could convert
the great Sophy of Persia![15]
I will make it possible
for you to get your way, my lord,
for I won't interfere, but instead
accept the friendship you offer me.
Let me know, if you will,   1300
how else I may be of service.

JUAN   Oh you ungrateful swine!

SANCHO   My lord!

JUAN   I am Don Juan—why are you so surprised?

SANCHO   What?

JUAN   You vile creature.
Is this how you see to your duty
and my honor? I'll kill you.

---

15   *Sophy*: The sovereign of Persia, an exonym for Iran.

DIEGO   What do you expect from such a fool?

SANCHO   Listen and you will see,   1310
             though you're so very angry,
             that my intentions were good.
             I recognized you at once,
             and since you seemed to be hiding,
             I decided to test you,
             to see whether you'd confess.

DIEGO   That is actually a good excuse.

SANCHO   Was I to go against my obligation
             for the sake of Don Diego,
             or even for the king,   1320
             as a loyal servant?
             Too bad for Don Diego!

JUAN   By taking his money,
             did you not undertake the obligation
             to help Don Diego?

SANCHO   I cannot deny it.
             Yet my plan was to take it
             and then to trick him.
             It's only right to repay
             betrayal with betrayal.   1330

JUAN   Oh you vile traitor, you liar!

SANCHO   Now what?

JUAN   See to what kind of man
             a noble gentleman offered his friendship!
             I am Don Diego de Luján.

SANCHO   Go away! By my life!
             Will this go on all day?
             "I'm Don Diego" and "I'm Don Juan!"

JUAN I am Don Diego,
yet to see if you were false, 1340
 I pretended to be Don Juan.

SANCHO And you think I don't know
you cannot be Don Juan?
I myself saw him on board,
and since I saw how you denied
being Don Diego, I did this
to make you confess.

JUAN A good excuse!

DIEGO A fine mess!

JUAN At least it's clear to one and all: 1350
whether I am called Luján or Castro,
I cannot put my trust in you.

SANCHO Whether you're Castro or Luján,
I serve you as best I can:
for you I deny Don Juan, if you're Don Diego,
Don Diego if you're Don Juan.
But if while I serve one of you,
 you plan to become the other,
then I won't bother to serve either,
so as not to offend anyone. 1360

SANCHO exits

DIEGO You've done it,
for now it's established
that *you* are *me*.

JUAN Nothing ventured, nothing gained, Don Diego.
But—oh, cousin!—console me
in my misfortune, for I die of it.
See how loyalty falters
at the first assault!

See how swiftly those defenses
surrendered! And Doña Ana,   1370
how easy, how fickle she was
in giving ear to my affections!

DIEGO   Only a fool sets out to test a woman.

JUAN   It might make sense if she's already his wife,
             but not when he has yet to marry her.

DIEGO   Don Juan, would it not be better
             to reveal yourself to our cousin,
             and, given that she values your love,
             to enjoy her love in peace?
             Doubt the most loyal of women   1380
             before testing her like this.
             Let her not say of you
             that you sought your own harm.
             What is the point of testing her,
             if you will only rue the day?
             Even if she proves disloyal,
             you would not be able to forget her.

JUAN   If she seems easy while I court her,
             I will know to guard her,
             even if I can't forget her.   1390
             Better to know what she is,
             though it pains me, and guard her,
             than to enjoy her without a care
             and lose my honor through her.

Enter INÉS

INÉS   All is ready, if you wish to rest.
             (*Aside*) I've never seen such a dapper servant.

DIEGO   (*Aside*) She's looking at me.

INÉS   There's water for your feet

with rosemary and roses in it.

JUAN Such attentions, young lady? 1400

INÉS Not lady, just Inés.

JUAN Well, good Inés, of the two of us,
you must take better care
of my servant there.

INÉS I will.
(*Aside*) I certainly care
more for him than for you.
(*Aloud*) Your beds are ready.

JUAN You are both lovely
and well-prepared. 1410

INÉS (*Aside*) How like Don Juan he looks!

Exeunt

SCENE 4

Sitting room in CELIO's *house*

Enter GERARDO *and* JULIA

GERARDO Listen to me, Julia.

JULIA Gerardo, please stop, by your life.

GERARDO How fiercely you suffer
in Leonardo's absence!

JULIA Whether I suffer or not
is no business of yours.
If I'm not concerned with your pain,

why should you care about mine?

GERARDO   My lady, while Leonardo was here   1420
            you listened more humanely,
            more patiently to my sad plaints.
            Yet since he's been gone,
            you have so despised me
            that it's as though
            I were the one who'd gone away.

JULIA   If you realize that, Gerardo,
            please stop, by your life!

GERARDO   I will enjoy you, you false woman,
            even if it pains you.   1430

JULIA   I'll scream.

GERARDO   Love undoes all my fear.
            It is useless to resist.

JULIA   What are you doing? Help, brother,
            for my honor is in danger!

                    Enter CELIO *with his sword drawn*

CELIO   What is this, Gerardo, you traitor!

GERARDO   Let go, you false woman!
            Celio, listen, it's your sister
            who offends you,
            while I look to your honor.   1440

                    GERARDO *unsheathes his sword*

JULIA   Brother!

GERARDO   Let me speak. Don't try any ploys.

JULIA   I already fear yours.
             This scoundrel tried to stain
             my honor by force.

GERARDO   Jesus! I see my fear of a trick
             was not in vain. Celio, listen to me.

JULIA   Brother, I'm telling the truth.
             Under the guise of friendship,
             he entered your house to wrong you.   1450

                         JULIA *exits*

CELIO   Traitor!

GERARDO   Before you jump to conclusions,
             hear me out and learn the truth.
             Julia was...
             But you won't believe what I have to say.
             Better to keep quiet and save my breath.

CELIO   Go on.

GERARDO   (*Aside*) What ruse can I devise?
             (*To* CELIO) Believe it or not,
             since you want to know,   1460
             the truth of the matter is
             I have courted Julia most properly,
             with all the respect due
             to our friendship and her honor.
             Then, you see, I discovered
             that a certain Don Diego de Luján,
             cousin and copy of that friend of yours,
             Don Juan de Castro,
             has been visiting and wooing her,
             and, what's more, she favors him.   1470
             I, in my jealousy,
             came to bid her love farewell.
             Either pained by my absence,

or just pretending to feel that way,
she took me by the arms
to calm my impatience.
But, since I was resolved
to quit her and make myself scarce,
she hit upon a false accusation
that would serve to keep me here—   1480
that I compromised her honor.
And that's how you found her,
claiming her honor was in jeopardy,
while I tried to free myself from her.
That is the truth. I am blameless.
Julia retains her honor.
Loving her was no betrayal,
and my jealous watch over her
was in your service.
Need I explain myself further?   1490

CELIO   You may need to,
if you are not being truthful,
so I will hold myself back
until I find out the truth.
Put away your sword and go.

GERARDO   (*Aside*) Blind Love,
why do you treat me this way?
The one time I take a chance,
her brother arrives on the scene?
But I can still make it work,   1500
if I stick to my story.

GERARDO exits

CELIO   Oh, the heavy burden of
trusting a woman's honor!

SCENE 5

On the street outside Julia's *house*

Enter Juan *and* Sancho

JUAN   If Inés loves Mendo instead of you,[16]
            I don't see what I can do.

SANCHO   I do.

JUAN   Tell me.

SANCHO   Dismiss Mendo,
            or you can say goodbye to me.

JUAN   Mendo has served me for years,   1510
            and I am much obliged to him.

SANCHO   I am just as obliged to Don Juan,
            and yet, by serving you,
            I have abandoned my obligation to him.

JUAN   But what was my servant's sin,
            if it was Inés who fell for him?

SANCHO   A fine excuse!
            Tell me: what was Don Juan's sin
            that justifies me offending him?
            Make this better at once,   1520
            or I will ruin your plans.
            See whether your heart prefers
            that servant over
            your cousin Ana's love.

Sancho *exits*

---

16   *Mendo*: the name that the real Don Diego takes on as a servant.

JUAN	Oh, what confusion,
	what pain these schemes lead to!

Enter DIEGO

DIEGO	What are you doing, cousin?

JUAN Don Diego,
a thousand strange torments
batter my peace of mind.   1530
Sancho has handed me an ultimatum:
either I must say goodbye to you,
or I can say goodbye
to his help with my love.

DIEGO Well, by my life!
They'll both be the death of me.
Sancho with his jealousy,
and Inés with her flirting.

JUAN That's the price
of being handsome.   1540

DIEGO We'll need to keep him quiet.

JUAN We'll talk about it later.
Here we are at Julia's house,
and I must give her
a letter that cost me
two thousand ducats.

DIEGO But wait:
see how the elegant dawn
emerges now from the house.

JUAN The sun rises to the world.   1550

Enter JULIA, *cloaked, and* GUILLÉN

JULIA   My lord, Don Juan!

JUAN   I am Don Diego de Luján,
           his cousin, and if you are Julia,
           my lady, I have something to tell you.

JULIA   I am Julia. Tell me, as long as it's brief.
           There's a wagging tongue
           at work against my honor.

JUAN   (*Gives her the letter*) Leonardo sends you
           this letter, and he wrote to me
           telling me...   1560

JULIA   Don Diego, goodbye.
           This is not the place.
           Find me at a better time.

JUAN   Yes, I will,
           if that is your command.

JULIA   It is.

JULIA *and* GUILLÉN *exit, with* DIEGO *following*

JUAN   Hello, Mendo! Mendo! Ah, Mendo!
           He follows her as if in a trance.
           Come back, Mendo!

JUAN *exits*

DIEGO   (*Offstage*) I fall from heaven   1570
           and return to hell.

SCENE 6

Room in RODRIGO's *house Enter* JUAN *and* DIEGO

DIEGO   God help me! What did I just see?
             That memory was dead,
             and now the past
             has been revived.

JUAN   What's happened?

DIEGO   Do not be surprised.
             When a man feels this way,
             there must be a reason.
             Doesn't Julia have a brother   1580
             named Celio?

JUAN   That is his name.

DIEGO   Hear what Love demands,
             hear what Time may do,
             the whims of Fortune,
             and what my misfortune
             has come to.
             You know, cousin,
             how young I was
             when I left for Flanders,   1590
             how I was much too young
             to even wear a sword.
             Since I could not serve Archduke Albert[17]
             on the battlefield,
             I entered his service as a page.
             The noble Julia served his wife then.
             Everyone died for her love
             and she gave life to me alone.
             She favored me so
             with tokens of affection   1600

---

17   Albert VII, Archduke of Austria, led several battles against French, English and Dutch troops between 1596-1604 to advance Spain's political power.

that I found myself
the envy of all Flanders, and rightly so.
It was either chance,
or my good looks,
or the fact that we lived together
in the same household
or that we were both children,
or that I was born lucky,
or that my cruel fortune   1610
wanted it so, to make my fall
all the more painful.
For when I least expected it,
as I enjoyed the spring of our love
and the roses in her cheeks,
after more than six years of love,
the unhappy news came that
her older brother had died
childless here in Spain.
The estate passed to Celio,   1620
who was in Flanders then,
expecting his reward
for a thousand feats in battle.
He decided to go back
to enjoy his income in peace,
taking Julia with him,
and a piece of my soul
along with her.
I devised a thousand ploys
and schemes to follow her   1630
—aided by Love, that mischievous child—
but none of them succeeded,
for the Archduke, my master,
enjoyed my service too well,
and, knowing my true reasons,
prevented my departure.
So, Julia and I said our goodbyes.
I can't express what I felt:
only one who has tasted
love and loss can understand it.   1640

We exchanged promises of love...
"Exchanged," did I say? Not quite.
My word was true,
while Julia, in the end,
spoke as a woman does.
She left. And just when I thought
I had defeated my terrible luck,
when I had a plan to free
myself from my master,
when I was ready to follow her,   1650
when I had gilded my green boots
with golden spurs and
put wings on a bay nag,
just then did loose-tongued Fame arrive
with the unhappiest of news:
Death had claimed both siblings.
A proud river,
swelling up to the sky,
extinguished the light
of this Diana, this Phoebus.[18]   1660
Consider the state I was left in.
What would my life be
without my beloved angel?
And so, I changed my plans.
I went to serve in the war,
where in six years I suffered
a thousand torments.
I secured a leave,
and came to Madrid
to seek favor at the court,   1670
and then to Seville to serve you,
only to find the mistress of my soul was here.
Is it then so unreasonable
to feel like I'm going mad,
when I find that my Julia is alive,
and I still feel as I ever did?

---

18   *Diana*: also known as Artemis, is a Greco-Roman goddess whose name
alludes to the Latin words for "sky" and "daylight." *Phoebus*: also known as Apollo, is
Diana's brother and the Greco-Roman god of the sun.

JUAN   Truly, your story is so strange
            that your reaction is no surprise.
            In fact, I am only surprised that
            you have not lost your mind.   1680
            I would congratulate you
            on finding her after all this time,
            but she loves Leonardo now,
            after disdaining him for so long.

DIEGO   Be quiet, for God's sake.
            That is much too harsh!

JUAN   What do you want? It's the truth,
            and the best friend is the one
            who is best at setting you straight.
            Besides, Leonardo, who went   1690
            all the way to Lima for my sake,
            charged me with watching over her,
            for he values her more than his soul.

DIEGO   And so what if he left her in your charge?
            Are you going to keep her from me?

JUAN   Cousin, you must understand
            my obligations here.

DIEGO   But I can be your excuse.

JUAN   And Leonardo is my excuse to you.

DIEGO   I am your cousin and your friend,   1700
            and Leonardo is just a friend.

JUAN   It's for that very reason
            that I owe more to him,
            absent though he is,
            for he has done me such a favor
            without even the bonds of kinship.

DIEGO   It's remarkable how kind I am to you,
given that we're family.
It's not how these things usually go,
for kindness in a kinsman is rarely found.   1710
Yet, of good friends, there are
a thousand famous examples.

JUAN   Have you ever known anyone
to give up his lady for his friend,
as Leonardo has done for me?

DIEGO   I have given up my very self!
For the sake of being your servant,
I am no longer who I was.
If you value his absence so,
know that I would do the same,   1720
if in doing so I served my cousin.

JUAN   You deny me the very thing
that I ask of you, and that I suspect
you know is what I need.

DIEGO   You do not ask me to absent myself,
as Leonardo has done,
you ask me to give up my lady
to another, for your sake.
Even asking for such a thing is unfair.
He would not do it, and neither will I.   1730

JUAN   I do not ask you to give her up,
but to let me watch over her
for the time being.

DIEGO   If I let you keep her from me,
it's the same as giving her up.

JUAN   I must keep my word.

DIEGO   And I will also keep

the word I have given you,
to help you pretend what you pretend.
And I will give my life for you1740
so that your love may come to fruition,
as you so desire, Don Juan.
But if you think that I will allow you
to keep Julia from me, by God,
know I will tear out the very soul of one
who seeks to take mine from me.

DIEGO *exits*

JUAN   Oh, to be caught in a web
of one's own deceit!
And the harms that follow
the first harm done!1750
I must keep my faith
and my word to Leonardo,
but if I keep it, Don Diego will resent me.
They both have a claim on me,
and I am obligated to them both.
As though my own troubles
were not enough on their own!

Enter INÉS

INÉS   Sir, what did you do to Mendo
that he looks so upset?

JUAN   I have scolded him on your account.1760

INÉS   On my account? I don't understand.

JUAN   I begged him to love you,
to make you happy;
yet he wouldn't budge
in the face of my pleas,
and he made me so angry
that I dismissed him at once.

INÉS   Have mercy on him, sir.

JUAN   Leave it.

INÉS   I burn for him.   1770
              If he stays dismissed,
              you can say goodbye to me.

JUAN   Inés, ask for anything else.

INÉS   When you deny me life itself,
              what else could I ask of you?
              This is what I deserve.

JUAN   Fine, then. I will do it
              to serve you, my dear Inés.

INÉS   There is more that you could do for me.

JUAN   Tell me.   1780

INÉS   Marry him to me.

JUAN   I can't make any promises,
              but I will certainly try.

INÉS   So it's the thought that counts?
              No. You must follow through.

JUAN   That's the very reason
              I had to dismiss him.
              Heaven itself cannot force
              a free will.

INÉS   If that's the case,   1790
              then I must appeal to your authority.
              Mendo esteems you so
              that he wishes only to please you;
              and since I'm playing the go-between
              for you with my lady,

I suggest you see to this.
For if you do not do as I wish,
I will tell my master Don Rodrigo
that you are wooing his niece.

Inés exits

Juan   How this house of cards shakes.   1800
Everyone conspires against it,
seeking to try my patience
and my sanity.

Enter Ana

Ana   (*Aside*) How vain it was to resist
your fire, oh blind Love!
Through Don Diego,
what power you have over me!
What star, what mighty planet
moves me and compels me,
against my will, so that I have loved you   1810
since the first moment I saw you?
Forgive this change of heart,
Don Juan, for if Don Diego has
conquered my heart, the arrow that
wounded me was your likeness.
(*To* Juan) Cousin!

Juan   Doña Ana, my dear...

Ana   What's troubling you?

Juan   The pain you cause me
so nobly suffered and so poorly paid,   1820
my dashed hopes
of conquering your coldness,
the unparalleled beauty that Nature
graced you with, beyond all belief,
so that my very life is death.

The glory that is Don Juan's
and the misfortune that is Don Diego's,
for the memory of him in his absence
crushes my present pleas.
How our story unfolds,   1830
how fate has led me
to such torments,
and how, in the end,
only death will bring me relief.

ANA   Have you no hope left?

JUAN   What hope could I have,
given your icy disposition
while I burn for you?

ANA   But disdain is just a step along the way
for one who prevails in the end.   1840
Happy endings work best
after a sad story,
and victory is sweeter
when hope is scarcer.

JUAN   If only I had some hope to hold onto,
I would consider myself
the luckiest man alive,
and second to none in my devotion.

ANA   There is no triumph without hope.

JUAN   There is no hope for one scorned,   1850
for he begins to doubt
his own merits.

ANA   No one need die of despair
who finds a sympathetic ear.

ANA *makes as if to leave*

JUAN   Come back, my darling,
            and speak your mind.
            Don't be shy, now.
            If there's happiness for me
            after such a sad story,
            do not deny me my victory.   1860
            If my love has conquered you,
            I beg you not to hide it.
            For to shower such favor upon me,
            Doña Ana, would be a sign of
            your nobility, and not your fickleness.

ANA   I don't know what to say, Don Diego.

JUAN   Well, I know what you should say to me.
            Say to me, my dear, that you repay
            my fire with sweet fire.

ANA   What my words would deny,   1870
            my actions confess,
            for they bear the mark
            of my amorous passion.
            The eyes speak for the heart.
            From the moment I found myself
            in your presence, Don Diego,
            I know not what resonance
            I felt inside my soul.
            I know not how I lost myself,
            for passion so forcefully overwhelmed me   1880
            that only through the miracle
            of my honest virtue
            have I managed to resist you.

JUAN   May I call you my very own?

ANA   A thousand times over.

JUAN   And Don Juan?

ANA   This is what he deserves
        for walking away from what he had.
        He must think very highly of himself
        to prolong his absence so.   1890
        Besides, you must understand
        what has produced this change of heart.
        It was your likeness to him
        that moved me in the first place.

JUAN   Enough, you deceptive,
        loose, fickle, false,
        lying, scheming, traitor!
        An inconstant sea battered
        by the winds, of two minds at least,
        a shrinking violet, wispy smoke   1900
        and trembling leaf,
        feather in the wind, ill-boding star,
        lightning bolt, demon.
        In short, a woman.
        I am Don Juan, and not Don Diego.
        All this is my doing,
        so I could find out the truth
        and see how blind I was.
        How soon that fire died out
        that once consumed you!   1910
        Were the tears that poured
        from you worth so little?
        Oh, pity the poor fool
        who trusts a woman's weeping!

ANA   Wait.

JUAN   No lie will serve you now.

ANA   Won't you listen to me?

JUAN   You will only try to deceive me.

ANA   I will show you how wrong you are.

1920

You have tried to trick me
and test my loyalty
with this fiction.
And I, well aware of this,
have set out to punish you
for the crime of testing me.

JUAN No. The honeyed words I heard
from your mouth were all too real.

ANA Of course they were real, Don Juan,
for I spoke them to you!

JUAN You spoke to me   1930
with the understanding that I was Don Diego.

ANA The fact is, I spoke those words to you,
whether you call yourself Diego or Juan.
A change in name
does not change the substance.[19]
I have loved the same body and soul
all along. How could I have betrayed
you with yourself?

JUAN By declaring your love for Diego
just now, when I am Juan.   1940

ANA If a simple name causes such outrage,
then it's only Juan's name
that need be jealous of Diego's.
But, you are you,
whether you call yourself Diego or Juan.
Don't drive yourself mad with abstract notions.
But if you must tighten the screws,
I will punish you too:
I say, in a nutshell,

---

19 Aristotelian philosophy held that form was analogous to the soul and matter analogous to the body. As Ana points out, Juan's name change does not reflect a material difference in his character because his soul remains the same.

that from this moment on,   1950
if you are Don Juan, I do not love you,
and if you are Don Diego, I do.
And to put an end to this nonsense
once and for all,
I will ask my uncle
to get to the bottom of this.

JUAN   Listen, here's the truth.

ANA   There's nothing to hear.

JUAN   Wait, cousin!

ANA   If you're Don Diego,   1960
            my love is yours, have no fear,
            but if you're Don Juan, then by God,
            it's off to Lima with you!

ACT III

SCENE 1

Room in Don Rodrigo's *house. Part of Don* Juan's *room is visible.*

Enter Juan *and* Celio

JUAN   I'm Don Diego de Luján.

CELIO   Don Diego, if I hadn't known
how much you look like him,
I might have taken you for Don Juan.

JUAN   I'm his cousin and the very image of him.

CELIO   I knew a Don Diego de Luján in Flanders,
and he looked nothing like you.   1970

JUAN   He too is my cousin,
and he wrote me today, in fact.
He's seeking favor at court in Madrid.

CELIO   For his wealth?

JUAN   For his service.

CELIO   May God grant him patience.

JUAN   Amen.

Enter ANA *and* INÉS *peeking through a door,*
without being seen by JUAN *and* CELIO

ANA   Celio looks upset.

INÉS   He looks like death itself.

ANA   Let's listen from here.   1980
I fear something is
seriously wrong.

CELIO   Do you know who I am?

JUAN   I've heard your name is Celio.

CELIO   Are you aware
I'm one of the most
respectable men in Seville?

JUAN   I'm well aware.

CELIO   Are you also aware
I have a sister   1990
renowned for her beauty?

JUAN   That's what I've heard.

CELIO   Well, that's why I'm here,
for I've heard you've been
visiting her in my absence.
If it is her hand you seek,
then you must speak with me.
But if your intention is to dishonor me,
then don't come near my house,
or set foot on my street,   2000
and you will have no trouble.

ANA   Oh, wretched traitor!

INÉS   Don't be surprised, my lady,
        if Don Diego behaves as all men do.

ANA   May the best of them burn in hell.

JUAN   I haven't entered your house
        since I set foot in Seville,
        and I declare that whoever
        told you otherwise is lying.
        Now that we've cleared that up,   2010
        you can trust my word
        that I will never cross that threshold.

CELIO   That is all I ask.

JUAN   I certainly owe you that much, Celio.

CELIO   I am much obliged.

JUAN   As I am to you.
        (*Aside*) This way I'll avoid offending
        both Leonardo and Don Diego.

CELIO exits

ANA *and* INÉS *still peeking through a door, without* JUAN *seeing them*

ANA   (*Aside*) My blood is boiling.
        (*Aloud*) Inés, what shall I do?   2020

INÉS   How should I know?
        Only a fool gives advice
        on matters of love.

ANA   You must help me find out
        the truth of the wrongs done to me.
        While I tell my cousin here
        of my woes, you go behind me
        and hide under his bed,

even if it means missing
a meal or two.   2030
See what he says when
he's alone with Mendo, Inés.

INÉS   I'll do it. Cover for me.
              I want to find out
              who this Mendo is,
              this disdainful, arrogant man
              who stinks of a gentleman.

            INÉS *leaves to find a hiding spot in* JUAN's *chambers*

                        ANA *walks toward* JUAN

JUAN   My dear cousin...

ANA   No more lies, you traitor!
              Put an end to your thousand treacheries,   2040
              your ploys and schemes.
              Now Don Diego, now Don Juan,
              now insolent, now gallant,
              now fictions, now facts.
              Be you Don Diego or Don Juan,
              what reason could you have
              for playing with me
              if it is Julia you want?
              Enough! I won't tolerate
              your schemes any longer.   2050
              Today I shall tell my uncle
              about your ruse,
              how you betrayed his trust
              and his hospitality.
              I'd already warned you once,
              but I listened to your pleas,
              or, rather, your ploys,
              since you only pretended to love me.
              I know full well you're Don Diego.
              The letters from your father make it clear.   2060

I read them myself.
If you ever thought I loved you,
you were sorely deceived.
I love Don Juan, and I only loved you
because you are the very image of him...
I do not love you, and were I to love you,
that would be the end of me!
Leave me be, you traitor!
I hardly know what I'm saying,
how could I ever say what I feel?   2070

ANA *exits*

JUAN   Wait, you false woman! You traitor!
You guarded Don Diego so jealously,
and now you pretend to burn
for Don Juan? How could you!
Had I put my trust in you
and actually gone away,
you'd have replaced me with
the first man who walked through the door.
Only a fool would expect a woman
to be more constant than the sea.   2080

SCENE 2

Enter SANCHO

SANCHO   Must you always be banging
your head against the wall?
Your fights always end
with you back together again.
I once met a gentleman at court, Don Diego,
who bickered with his lady every morning,
swearing he would never see her again,
only to sleep with her every night.
For six years they fought like this,
if for no other reason   2090

than not to lose the habit.
If you love each other
and are already halfway down the aisle,
why must you always get along
like oil and water?

JUAN   Oh if she loved me...

SANCHO   Oh if the Sophy of Persia could make
all my wishes come true...[20]

JUAN   Wouldn't Inés be better?

SANCHO   ...then he could make me a Persian Pasha,   2100
the Sophy's confidant,
and then maybe Inés would love me too...

JUAN   Well, you'd be a Moor, so she probably wouldn't,
because she's Christian.

SANCHO   Good point. But what woman
wouldn't convert at once
for power and money?
As a poet once said,
"Marry a Moor for money,
and a Christian for nothing."[21]   2110
Although actually,
that last one is not quite true,
for if a Christian has no money,
women want nothing to do with him.
The one who longs
to attend Mass each Sunday
doesn't do it for Christ,
but for the men in church.
I have met more than one
well-versed in the latest fashions,   2120

---

20   Sancho seems to be mocking Juan for his lovesick behavior.
21   A refrain from the *Romancero,* a collection of medieval ballads popular
during the 14th and 15th centuries.

yet when asked to recite the Lord's Prayer,
she only gets as far as "our daily bread."
The one with a rosary in hand
is not counting Hail Marys,
but figuring out how much
she'll take you for.

JUAN   You're being cynical, Sancho.

SANCHO   Who, me? I never!

JUAN   Then you'll get what's
coming to you.   2130

SANCHO   A chat without gossip
is like a sangria without the orange.

JUAN   Carping makes for a tasty dish,
but it doesn't come cheap.

SANCHO   So tell me, what's with this Mendo fellow?

JUAN   He swears you have nothing
to be jealous of, no matter how
much Inés pursues him.

SANCHO   You just want to distract me
with false promises.   2140

JUAN   Go into that room
and see for yourself
how much I trust Mendo.
He's never been the root of my anger.

SANCHO   No winking at each other now,
or secret signs amongst yourselves.
I know all the tricks.

JUAN   Here he comes—go hide, go.

SANCHO *goes into* JUAN's *room, while* INÉS *hides behind the bedcurtains*
Enter DIEGO

JUAN   I was looking for you, Mendo.

DIEGO   At your service.   2150
                (*Aside*) He called me Mendo—
                there must be someone listening.

JUAN   Mendo, you know how Celio has been acting so jealous?

DIEGO   Jealous? Tell me more.
                Who is he jealous of?

JUAN   Of me.

DIEGO   Well, what has he heard about you?

JUAN   Something that will bring us
                to blows if I tell the truth.   2160
                He said...

They lower their voices while SANCHO, *without being seen,*
is searching the room

SANCHO   One by one, I discovered
                a barrel of olives,
                a jug and a cask of wine.
                I can't help it, it tastes so good!

He drinks

                At least I'll have one for the road.
                I've made a nice dent in it.
                I'll just lie here and watch.
                I'm going to hold on tight.
                Feeling a little woozy now.   2170
                Maybe I should sit
                and make myself comfortable.

Now that I think about it,
I'll just lie down.

He lies down behind a bed

(*Slurring*) Effvryfing is getting blurry.
I'll close my eyes.
Oh damned sleep,
what do you want from me?

He falls asleep

JUAN   ...And then we left it at that,
            for Celio was satisfied   2180
            with my answer.

DIEGO   And I am as well,
            because I got my wish.
            As I see it, you are no longer
            obliged to concern yourself
            with Julia.

SANCHO *snores*

JUAN   Never mind that now.
            What's that noise?

They go into JUAN's *room*

DIEGO   It's Sancho asleep
            behind your bed.   2190

JUAN   Oh, what a vigilant spy!
            He hid there to see
            how I would confront you
            about Inés for his sake.

DIEGO   What should we do?
            What if I trip over him?

JUAN   Make it hurt.

              DIEGO *steps on* SANCHO, *who wakes up, stands,*
                  and pulls on the bedcurtain, revealing INÉS

SANCHO   San Miguel,
              San Onofre, San Gonzalo,
              San Custodio, San Mamés,   2200
              San Inocente, San Pablo!
              I beg of you, the devil got me!

INÉS   No, Sancho, it's just me.

SANCHO   Jesus protect me from evil!

JUAN   Wake up!

SANCHO   God be with me!

DIEGO   What's wrong? Tell us.

SANCHO   I'll tell you.
              I was dreaming of Judgement Day.

JUAN   And what did you see?   2210

SANCHO   Let me tell you.
              High on a court bench
              sat a tailor and a squire
              who came to judge
              the living and the dead.

JUAN   What nonsense!

SANCHO   It's not nonsense!
              When a tailor takes a man's measure
              and makes his cutting remarks,
              isn't that like the Last Judgement?   2220
              What life, good or bad,

is safe from a squire
trading gossip with his mates
while they all wait for their masters?
The tailor and squire wanted
to hand down their judgement,
so they hatched a plan to make
everyone, dead or alive,
report at once.
And it was a neat trick, too: 2230
instead of sounding a trumpet,
they just jangled some coins.
As soon as they heard,
all the dead left their graves,
though of course the women
got there faster.
It was something to see,
how the souls returned to their bodies.
Some did not like what they saw
and refused to return.   2240
Others diligently searched
for every missing fingerbone…
One old woman, annoying me to death,
asked after her lost teeth.
A fat innkeeper
with a missing buttcheek
finally found the other half
inside a baker's oven.
A lady of the night
who died by drowning   2250
could not recognize her own face
without the makeup,
and yet her face was washed
as she went to her judgement.
Another one never thought
she could lose face,
and yet a swarm of flies
found her all the sweeter
for her pancake.
In the middle of all this,   2260

a woman dragged herself by
with both legs broken.
An unrepentant thief
had stolen her good ones,
as was his old habit.
She made her pitiful case.
The judges that heard it
said, "All women's legs
should be broken, if only
to keep them at home."   2270
But they left it at that,
for they soon turned to
a thief and scribe madly
fighting over an eye:
the thief needed a lookout,
the scribe an eyewitness.
The tailor weighed in at once,
giving them both an earful and
keeping the eye for himself.
"The tailor needs as many   2280
eyes as he can get," a poet once said,
"one per needle!"
But he was soon punished
for his painful puns.
No sooner was he summoned
than they sent him to the stake
for his biting satire,
and burned him with
a thousand bad plays.
But he who is happy to burn   2290
as long as he has the last word said,
"You're using bad plays?
There's no lack of fuel then."[22]
A certain lady in a coach
was accused of spending
the entire night with a man
whom she didn't love.

---

22   Alludes to the prodigious creative output of Spanish playwrights during
the sixteenth and seventeenth centuries.

She replied, "Though I had no satisfaction,
thinking of the benefaction
that he'd hand over in the morning   2300
made it all worthwhile."
To teach her a lesson,
they condemned her
to spend the rest of eternity
embraced by a man with bad breath
who wouldn't stop kissing her.
Arguing that he could get more
out of her in this world,
the devil refused to drag her
down to the world below.   2310
But a wise guy said,
"You'd better get her out of here,
for every man who sleeps with her
repents and changes his ways after."
Then came a so-called Lady Maria,
wife to my Lord Grocer,
but the squire soon dubbed her
"Maria Plain and Square."
Then came an old lady
made up in youthful fashion,   2320
and they beat her over the head
with the weight of her years.
There came a gluttonous man
who served himself
with a liberal hand.
They stuck him with a cook:
with one hand she took,
but never gave with the other.
Then came one who through mishap
ended up working on her back.   2330
She was sentenced to wander
dragging her deadbeat clients
wherever she might go.
An old man who covered his grey hair
with all manner of dyes
was sentenced to reveal

his true colors to one and all.
A hot-headed man who was
always needling others
was condemned to embroidery   2340
and the most intricate needlepoint.
A crooked old go-between
on the lookout for marks
was condemned to find
only soldiers and students,
the brokest of the broke.
Then came one who'd rashly married young.
The only reason he was spared
was that he pretended not to see
the spare men in his wife's bed.   2350
After him, it was my turn.
And for my wicked, wicked vice
of drinking like this,
they had a slippery old devil
saddle me with casks of ...water.
I felt them here, on my poor back.
It hurt so much it woke me up.
And when I saw Inés there,
so close to my face,
I cried for the devil to take me: 2360
the lesser of two evils.

INÉS   So I'm the devil now,
and not "My angel this
and my angel that."

SANCHO   An angel because I love you,
but a devil because you tempt me so.

JUAN   Well, Madam Inés, what were you
doing behind my bed?

DIEGO   So my privacy is a casualty
of Sancho's lovelife.   2370

INÉS   You should burn him instead.

DIEGO   Amen.

SANCHO   Don't "amen" me, Master Mendo.
Don't you see you are speaking
to a well-mannered man.

JUAN   That's enough.

SANCHO   Yes, that is enough.

JUAN   Let Inés say what she was doing.

INÉS   Sancho keeps following me,
so when I saw him coming,   2380
I tried to shake him off.

SANCHO   By God, that's a pretty story!
The truth is we were both
hiding there so Mendo wouldn't see us.
That's who Inés is hiding from.

DIEGO   That is indeed the truth.

INÉS   The scoundrel lies.

SANCHO   Liar, just save your breath.

JUAN   Hand me my cloak and sword.

INÉS   What vile lies!   2390

JUAN   Enough.

JUAN speaks with SANCHO to the side

I turned Inés over to you
on a silver platter.

SANCHO	And then I made sure
	she turned against Mendo.

JUAN *speaks with* DIEGO *to the side*

JUAN	I'm about to explode.
	Come, cousin,
	I'm dying to tell you...

INÉS	Mendo...

DIEGO	Why does she call to me?	2400
	Does the little liar want to tell us
	what she dreamt of while hiding
	with Sancho behind the bed?

INÉS	Is this how I am to be treated,
	 and all because of you,
	you despicable lout?
	I swear to God, you'll pay for this,
	you snake.

Exeunt

SCENE 3

Enter JULIA, *holding a letter, and* GUILLÉN

JULIA	Guillén, watch the door
	while I go over this letter.	2410
	I don't want Celio to see it.

GUILLÉN	I will look out for him and all other dangers.

GUILLÉN *exits*

JULIA	Oh my dying hopes,
	the bane of my existence.

Where do these hopes lead me,
pursuing a happiness that escapes me,
taking me to a place where time and space
will erase all memory of me?
What strange twists love follows,   2420
always down the darkest paths!

Reads the letter
Enter DIEGO *and* GUILLÉN

GUILLÉN   You've come just in time.
            She is finishing her reply to Leonardo now.
            I'm watching the door for Celio.

DIEGO   (*Aside*) I'm burning with jealousy.
            (*Aloud*) Keep watching, then,
            while I give my message to Julia.

GUILLÉN   Be quick, Mendo.

GUILLÉN *exits*

DIEGO *takes the letter from* JULIA

DIEGO   Fickle traitor!

JULIA   What's this? How dare you!   2430
            Guillén!

DIEGO   Go ahead, call away.
            I'm ready to meet
            my untimely death.
            Don't you know who I am?

JULIA   My God! Can it be?
            Don Diego de Luján!

JULIA *reaches out to him*

Diego   Stop, you traitor!
             Do not reach for me
             with that faithless hand,   2440
             the very hand that you once gave me,
             covered with your tears.
             And now it writes to another,
             another absent lover,
             and signs your name
             to your disloyalty and my injury.
             Oh, heavens above!
             Is it not just to seek vengeance
             against a traitorous hand?
             How can I burn so when I am blameless,   2450
             while the sinner can't even smell the smoke?
             What of your promises, you liar?
             What of the heavenly witnesses
             you invoked, who must now
             denounce you for the promise you made,
             binding yourself to me,
             "til' death do us part?"
             You barely knew the one
             you entrusted with your very soul!
             Yet I, though I had given up hope   2460
             of your being alive,
             never broke any of my promises.
             And you, who made so many,
             could not keep a single one?
             In the end, you acted
             just like any other woman.
             Be Leonardo's then.
             Let him come to the same end!
             He will, you know,
             since you're the one who loves him.   2470

                            Diego *exits*

Julia   Wait, come back, stay!
             My first love, I was always yours.
             Listen to me at least.

Would you have me die
without hearing my plea?
What inhuman judge would condemn me to this?

Enter GUILLÉN

GUILLÉN   Why so sad, Julia?

JULIA   Follow Don Diego at once.

GUILLÉN   Which Don Diego?

JULIA   The one that just left.   2480

GUILLÉN   Calm down.

JULIA   Go after him, Guillén.
             Find out where he lives.

GUILLÉN   Hold your horses, now,
             that was Mendo who just left.

JULIA   Right! Clearly you know exactly what's going on!

GUILLÉN   I don't understand you.
             His name is Mendo.
             Don Diego de Luján,
             who gave you Leonardo's letter,   2490
             is his master.

JULIA   (*Aside*) This is either a dream
             or a scheme about to be revealed.
             (*Aloud*) Where does your Don Diego live?

GUILLÉN   He's staying with his uncle,
             Don Rodrigo de Castro.

JULIA   (*Aside*) Oh my love, the ember
             of your amorous fire still burns,

although the long days
rained cold ashes upon it.   2500
Your love was the first wound
Cupid gave me.
It is madness to blame one
who changed her heart
only when she had lost all hope
of having you again.
But now that I see you are still in love,
You'll see that my change of heart
was like drawing back the bow
so the arrow would fly true.   2510
And so my love is renewed.
(*Aloud*) Guillén, on our way to mass tomorrow,
I'll go to Don Diego's house.

GUILLÉN   You will put us at risk.

JULIA   Are you trying to hold me back?
                 You don't understand.
                 The more you try to stop me,
                 the more determined I am to go.

GUILLÉN *and* JULIA *exit*

SCENE 4

On the street

Enter CELIO *and* GERARDO

CELIO   Gerardo, I have been unable
                 to find out the truth   2520
                 given the confusion in my house.
                 My sister and Don Diego
                 deny what you say is true,
                 while I would swear on our friendship
                 that their claim is false.

And so, to avoid further investigation,
we should just remove the occasion
for any further offense.
Don Diego has given me his word:
he will not set foot in this house again. 2530
You must do the same.

GERARDO   Your request is so reasonable
that I'll gladly comply,
though I must say I regret
I can't do more to convince you.
I regret you have come to suspect my loyalty.
I regret to see our friendship
ruined for no reason.

CELIO   Not necessarily, Gerardo, my friend,
but it's up to you. 2540
We can remain friends,
if you do as I say.
If you are a true friend,
you will agree to this too:
you will no longer visit my sister.
If you value my friendship
as highly as you claim,
you'll oblige me one more time
by doing as I say.

GERARDO   Rest assured that 2550
my affection is such
that I will show my loyalty,
by looking to your honor.

CELIO   I never expected anything less of you, Gerardo.

GERARDO   Anything for you.
I am at your service.

CELIO   Go with God.

GERARDO   May God be with you.

Exit CELIO

GERARDO   I swear to God, Julia, my enemy,
               that I'll watch over you   2560
               like Argos of the hundred eyes.
               You won't take a step
               without me following you.
               I'm burning up,
               and I'll show your brother I was right.
               It's no coincidence that I twice saw
               Don Diego at your door.
               Since you leave me with no hope,
               I will turn my love into penalty.
               A hopeless love always   2570
               appeals to vengeance.

Exit GERARDO

SCENE 5

A room in RODRIGO's *house*

Enter INÉS *and* SANCHO

INÉS   Your affection offends me, Sancho,
               and all your pleading.
               What is it you want?
               My heart belongs to Mendo,
               and I owe him all my love.

SANCHO   That only makes my suit the worthier.
               If you weren't so hard to get,
               I wouldn't be in so deep.

INÉS   And Mendo, how would he feel   2580
               if I were to be your lady?

Would you be happy
if I treated you that way?

SANCHO   No, of course not, Inés.
But I'm not courting you
for Mendo's sake, but for mine.

INÉS   Here comes Don Diego.
I wouldn't want Mendo
to see me with you.

Exit INÉS

SANCHO   May God punish you,   2590
and make you a hag overnight,
your skin rougher than a crocodile
and your wrinkles crevices
where bed bugs breed!

Enter JUAN *and* DIEGO

JUAN   What's going on, Sancho?

SANCHO   It's Inés, my master,
who, by all that is good in heaven,
not only makes me jealous,
but won't allow my love.

DIEGO   That takes the cake!   2600

JUAN   I understand.
Where are you going?

SANCHO   I must leave you, Don Diego.
I've had it with Mendo's secrets.

SANCHO *exits*

JUAN   Any news of Julia since yesterday?

DIEGO What could have happened since yesterday?

JUAN What, haven't you been back
  since yesterday?

DIEGO And what would it mean to go back?

JUAN You know, it wouldn't be so strange   2610
  to move on after six years apart,
  and all the more
  since your letters stopped coming.

DIEGO I thought she was dead.
  That's my excuse.

       SANCHO *comes back*

SANCHO My master, here comes Julia.

DIEGO Who?

SANCHO Julia. She is already at the door.

    Enter JULIA, *cloaked, and* GUILLÉN

JUAN You in this house, my lady?
  I must be dreaming.   2620

JULIA Throw your niceties out the window.
  Desperate times call for desperate measures,
  and I'm in such a state...

JUAN Wait, our servants need not
  know your troubles.
  Sancho and Guillén, go away.

SANCHO And what about Mendo?
  Doesn't he have a tongue?

JUAN   Don't talk back.

SANCHO   (*Aside*) At least Inés isn't staying.   2630

                    Exit SANCHO *and* GUILLÉN

JUAN   This way I needn't fear
              that Sancho will reveal
              our scheme.

DIEGO   That was a smart move.

JULIA   Don Diego, I am not here
              to appeal to you,
              for if remembrance has no hold over you,
              what would be the point?
              I'm here to answer for my honor.
              Your rude accusations have   2640
              offended my reputation.
              Seven years have passed since
              I came here from Flanders,
              leaving behind my soul and my liberty,
              for they remained with you.
              In all these long years,
              I haven't heard from you.
              Isn't this obvious proof
              that you have forgotten me?
              What could be clearer?   2650
              In the absence of all hope,
              I took on a new love.
              It's not fickleness to seek
              a port in a storm.
              If a master chooses to dismiss his servant,
              he cannot possibly be offended
              when that servant seeks
              a new master to serve.
              Be glad that when I saw you again,
              I showed you my affection.   2660
              Any other loves were misguided.

Be glad that I love you once again
now that my hopes are rekindled.
My change of heart was only due to despair.

Enter Sancho

SANCHO Be glad that Leonardo is here,
even now in the entryway.

JULIA Leonardo?

SANCHO The one who followed Don Juan,
my master, to the New World.

JULIA How can that be? 2670

SANCHO He can answer that himself.
Here he is.

JULIA Oh no!

JUAN Julia, you must hide.
Don't make this any worse.

Julia *exits*

DIEGO (*Aside*) I am out of my mind with jealousy.

Enter Leonardo

SANCHO I bow before you, Leonardo.

LEONARDO Sancho!

SANCHO Where is my master, Don Juan?

LEONARDO He is sailing in good health. 2680

SANCHO This is Don Diego de Luján
you see in his place.

Leonardo   Give me your arms, Don Diego.

Juan   And my heart!
           The only reason I did not come out
           to greet you was because
           I thought Sancho must be joking
           when he said you were here.

Leonardo   Heaven willed
           what I thought was impossible.   2690

Juan   How so?

Leonardo   We left the great bay
           with a good wind at our back,
           and soon lost sight of Spain
           beyond the sea.
           For fifteen days the sun's rays
           lit the ocean waves with a silvery sparkle
           as our fleet smoothly tilled
           the fields of Neptune.
           Then, the final hour of my journey came.   2700
           One morning when the sun laid
           its carpet of gold and red threads
           for the dawn to tread on,
           all at once a sharp sorrow,
           a rude awakening,
           turned my soft bed into thorns.
           I couldn't help it, I fled from my thoughts
           and rushed to the deck.
           I sat on the edge, a solitary lover
           facing the sky, feet in the water,   2710
           when in an instant the ship rocked,
           its side plunging into the icy waves.
           And I, a wretched and green sailor,
           unprepared for that sudden danger,
           was not even holding on,
           and fell into the water.
           The momentum plunged me

deep into the sea.
I wildly thrashed about,
swimming as best I could   2720
and hoping each stroke would save my life.
But when I finally burst through
the frigid waters and into the air above,
I saw my haven swiftly receding,
flying on the wind,
and turning its back on my cries.
Three hundred men aboard
and every last one deaf to my misfortune!
Perhaps Dawn sprinkled a sleeping potion
in her precious tears that morning,   2730
so that they slept like the dead.
Or perhaps it was just my leeward fall,
my cries dying on the wind.
I lost sight of the ship.
Imagine the state I was in!
With no hope of human help,
I appealed to God instead
with vows and promises.
His merciful hand sent a boat
on its way back to Spain.   2740
When they spotted me, its noble passengers
fished me out and brought me back to land.
Then I made my way to see you.

JUAN   I congratulate you on your safe arrival.

Enter GUILLÉN, *upset*

GUILLÉN   What is taking you so long, Julia?

JUAN   What is this, Guillén?

GUILLÉN   My lady must hide, Celio is on his way.

JUAN   Are you out of your mind?

Enter CELIO *and* GERARDO

CELIO Killing her
would be a kindness, Gerardo. 2750

GERARDO You shall see my truth.

GUILLÉN (*Aside*) I shall hide here.

GUILLÉN *exits*

LEONARDO (*Aside*) Have I been betrayed somehow?

JUAN (*Aside*) What shall I do now?

SANCHO (*Aside*) Troy will burn tonight.[23]

CELIO Don Diego, you have failed
to keep your promise,
and broken the vow you made,
hand on heart, not to pursue my sister.
Only a scoundrel would do such a thing. 2760

JUAN Celio, this is not the place
to punish such boldness,
for we are in my uncle's house,
which I must respect.
Meet me out in the fields.
There you shall have satisfaction.

CELIO Hold on! Is this a scheme
to get rid of me?
First you must hand over Julia,
whom you have hidden away, Don Diego. 2770
Then I shall take your life.

---

23 *Troy will burn tonight*: idiomatic expression indicating a looming disaster
(see note 11).

JUAN   What do you mean? I don't understand.

CELIO   You cannot deny it. I saw Guillén
              sneaking in here with my own eyes.
              Hand over Julia, or by God I will
              set fire to this house!

LEONARDO   If that is the case, hand her over, Don Diego.

GERARDO   You, here, Leonardo?

LEONARDO   I am.

GERARDO   First Julia, and now you?   2780

CELIO   Enough. Let Julia come with us.
              I will not leave without her...
              I'll take your life instead.

              Enter RODRIGO, ANA *and* INÉS

RODRIGO   Heavens! Why all this commotion?

ANA   (*To* INÉS) This does not bode well, Inés.

INÉS   (*Aside*) Little do you know.
              (*To* ANA) I'm trembling with fear.

RODRIGO   What is this Celio?
              Such scandal in my house?

JUAN   Celio has been misinformed.   2790

CELIO   Do not be so surprised, Don Rodrigo.
              Don Diego has robbed me of my honor
              by seeking my sister's favor
              and then concealing her in your very house.
              You tell me whether I should protect

my reputation, or die trying.

RODRIGO   What do you say to this, nephew?
JUAN   I deny Celio's claims.

GERARDO   There's no use denying it.
            I saw her go in, Don Diego,   2800
            and she has not come out.

JUAN   Have you been watching her?

GERARDO   My honor required it.

RODRIGO   Calm down, I will go inside
            and look for her. I give you my word,
            Celio, that if I find her,
            I will bring her out here,
            so that Don Diego
            restore your honor at once
            by making Julia his wife.   2810

CELIO   That is the only way out.

RODRIGO *exits*

ANA *speaks separately to* INÉS

ANA   Can you believe that!
            Don Diego's love for me was all a lie.

LEONARDO   (*Aside*) Can it be that Don Juan
            loved Julia all along?
            By God, he is a traitor.
            He sent me to the Indies
            so he could court her himself!

JUAN   (*Aside*) Damn that woman.
            She's ruined all my schemes.   2820

Enter JULIA, RODRIGO *and* GUILLÉN

RODRIGO   Julia, come out here with me.
You have nothing to fear...

JULIA   I wish I were dead!

RODRIGO   Love always leads us astray.

GUILLÉN   (*Aside*) It's all over now, Guillén.

ANA   (*Aside*) Could such a thing be true?

CELIO   See how my house is dishonored!

LEONARDO   (*Aside*) Since she hid from me,
it certainly wasn't me she was looking for.
My worst fears have come true,   2830
but I will say nothing until this is over.

JULIA   (*Aside*) I'm so embarrassed.

CELIO   Will you now deny, Don Diego,
the wrong you did to my honor?

JUAN   Celio, if I had offended you,
I would give you satisfaction.
But Julia has come to my house
seeking news of Leonardo,
who has miraculously
returned here today.   2840
Why are you condemning me for this?

CELIO   Is this true?

JULIA   It is true.

DIEGO   (*Aside*) What to do?

Don Juan, by not revealing himself,
risks all my good fortune.

LEONARDO Well tell me, false Julia,
who are you trying to fool?
If you were here looking for me,
why did you hide? 2850

JULIA I wanted to hide so I could listen in
and find out whether your love was true.

CELIO Give her your hand, Leonardo,
and thus restore my honor.
Julia is your equal
in wealth and nobility.

DIEGO (*Aside*) May Don Juan forgive me.
I cannot wait any longer.
(*Aloud*) Celio, what you have been
Told here is all a ruse. 2860
Julia came to see me.

GERARDO Is this a joke or madness?

DIEGO I am Don Diego de Luján.
This is no joke.
Celio, you know me well
from when we lived in Flanders.

CELIO I know you like the back of my hand.

DIEGO Your sister has been my wife
ever since Flanders,
which she confirmed by her letters, 2870
her words, her favors,
and other more irrevocable pledges.
Don Juan de Castro is now in a bind,
and so he invents what he must,
in order to keep up his disguise.

	He remained at	
	home pretending to be me:	
	such are the schemes that love demands.	
	But, given that I am about to lose	
	what I treasure most,	2880
	I must break my vow of silence.	
	Whatever happens to Don Juan,	
	his father will make sure	
	he lands on his feet.	

RODRIGO   What! Are you Don Juan?

JUAN   I am Don Juan.

SANCHO   This is like a play!

RODRIGO   Well tell me: what possessed you
to hatch this intricate plot?

JUAN   Love is to blame.   2890
My cousin Ana had struck me
with her tainted love arrows,
and so, I feigned what you have heard,
in order to remain here.
Would that I had not done so,
for her fickleness has served
to punish my misdeed!

ANA   Don Juan, you blame me for no reason.
I cannot betray you with yourself.
Stop this vain quibbling.   2900
Heaven has granted our natures
a natural affinity:
changing your name
could not change that.
And so, I blindly followed my stars,
from which you must conclude
that I cannot love anyone, besides you.
And since it's time to speak the truth,

	you should know that as soon as
	Don Diego came to your house 2910
	he told me who he was,
	but I kept quiet, because he had
	entrusted me with his secret.
	And so, I have always loved you
	as Don Juan. Don Diego can be
	my witness.

DIEGO   (*Aside*) She is my cousin, so I will help her.
She clearly wants me to go along with her story.
(*Aloud*) Don Juan, Doña Ana speaks the truth.
She adores you and cherishes you   2920
as Don Juan. Give her your hand,
for her devotion merits it.

JUAN   Although you betrayed me
by revealing my secret,
I am glad to hear that
Doña Ana has not been untrue,
and so I give her my hand,
as long as my father agrees.

RODRIGO   Doña Ana is also of my blood,
and I am happy to see her wed,   2930
but surely you cannot marry your cousin
without a dispensation?

JUAN   I have seen to that.
Love never sleeps.

CELIO   So I'm just here to
celebrate your wedding.

DIEGO   If Julia will have me,
you can be part of that one too.

JULIA   It's my great fortune.

DIEGO	Cheer up, Leonardo.	2940
	In the game of love,	
	the first move always wins.	
LEONARDO	I cannot stand in your way,	
	since when I was lost at sea	
	I pledged myself to God,	
	if only he would save me.	
SANCHO	Thank God, sister Inés,	
	there is no more Mendo to worry about.	
	You must give me your hand,	
	even if you don't want to.	2950
INÉS	I do want to. Play on, Sancho.	
SANCHO	Play along, Sancho?	
	Is that what you expect of a husband,	
	to play along with your games?	
	Keep away from me.	
INÉS	*Play on*, I said.	
SANCHO	Play on then,	
	and here ends our play.	